Christa Black

GOD LOVES UGLY

& love makes beautiful

Faith Words

NEW YORK BOSTON NASHVILLE

Graphic Artwork: Libby Gifford
Photography: Steven Taylor
Styling & Makeup: Tasha Homan for Relevant Hair
Hair: Carmody Homan for Relevant Hair, and Lynn Dowling

Unless otherwise indicated, all scripture quotations are taken from the New American Standard Bible (Copyright © 1960, 1962, 1963, 1971, 1972, 1973, 1975, 1977, 1995 by the Lockman Foundation). Scripture taken from *The Message*. Copyright © 1993, 1994, 1995, 1996, 2000, 2001, 2002. Used by permission of NavPress Publishing Group. Scripture taken from The Holy Bible, New International Version® NIV®. Copyright © 1973, 1978, 1984, 2011 by Biblica, Inc.™. Used by permission.

All rights reserved worldwide.

The author has added italics to scripture quotations for emphasis and all emphasis within scripture quotations is the author's own.

FaithWords
Hachette Book Group
1290 Avenue of the Americas
New York, NY 10104
www.faithwords.com

Printed in the United States of America

RRD-C

Originally published in hardcover by Hachette Book Group.

First trade edition: June 2013

10 9 8 7 6 5

FaithWords is a division of Hachette Book Group, Inc.
The FaithWords name and logo are trademarks of Hachette Book Group, Inc.

The Hachette Speakers Bureau provides a wide range of authors for speaking events. To find out more, go to www.hachettespeakersbureau.com or call (866) 376-6591.

The publisher is not responsible for websites (or their content) that are not owned by the publisher.

ISBN 978-1-4555-1658-2 (pbk.)

Praise for **GOD LOVES UGLY**

"I wish I had this book when I was struggling with bulimia as a teenage girl. Thank you, Christa, for presenting your story with such raw vulnerability and honesty. You show that true beauty comes from what seems like the ugliest secrets. Freedom will be experienced by many as a result. And as the mom of three girls, I promise I will be referencing this book often."

—Natalie Grant, award-winning singer-songwriter

"This book is for anyone who has ever wanted to be loved. It's not just for people in despair or rehab; it's a dose of loving truth for us all. I can attest to this awakening in Christa's life...I've seen it up-close and beautiful! This beauty-for-ashes story will never grow old."

—Christy Nockels, singer-songwriter,
part of the 268 generation

"Brilliantly written, real, raw, inspiring. Christa is a true role model who has an amazing story to share and teach from."

—Pattie Mallette, author of *Nowhere But Up:
The Story of Justin Bieber's Mom*

"If ever there was a book worth reading and a journey worth taking, it is this one. Christa has a remarkable way of putting her heart on paper. GOD LOVES UGLY will encourage you to search your own life and rediscover truth, beauty and how love changes everything. Whether you're nine or 109, the words in these pages will teach you to see with new eyes."

—Kari Jobe, worship leader, songwriter

"'God Loves Ugly' is a song that changed my life and self-esteem, and now GOD LOVES UGLY is a book that inspired my heart."
—Jordin Sparks, *American Idol* winner

"Christa really hit the bulls-eye with GOD LOVES UGLY. I can't wait to give this book to my mom, sister, and every other woman in my life. It's extremely relatable and encouraging."
—Kellan Lutz, actor

"I can't recommend this book enough. Christa's effortless style and honesty will reach hearts, inspiring hope for all who struggle to believe true freedom is for them."
—Michael W. Smith, Grammy-winning artist

"Intelligent, creative, humble, generous, passionate, raw, and honest…these are some of the words that spring to mind while reading this wonderful piece of heartfelt literature by my friend, Christa Black. As she delves into subject matter that is often danced around, she has the grace to give each of us readers real life stories, with real life answers in a way that empowers and brings light rather than shame. I am confident that this book will be life changing *and* life saving for so many, and my heart is ever grateful for the courage and tenacity of our beautiful Christa. Be inspired as you read."
—Darlene Zschech

"After reading GOD LOVES UGLY, one word kept echoing through my mind and heart: compassion. Christa courageously peels back the layers of fear and defense mechanisms to reveal a heart created to receive love and live a life of compassion. Battling the lies that try to guide our beliefs is a part of my story and the story of countless others. Christa shares keys to freedom from the lies and like a true friend, leads you down the path to total joy and deliverance. You won't be disappointed!"
—Kim Walker-Smith, Jesus Culture

"This book is a beautiful portrait of the Father's heart for us. I love how Christa exposes the lies of beliefs that disempower. She does a great job of teaching people to know who they are and how the Father sees them."
—Jenn Johnson, Bethel Music

To my life partner and Studhubs, Lucas. Your love continues to heal me deeper than any earthly medicine ever could. I learn from your compassionate heart, peaceful demeanor, and stoic wisdom every single day. Thank you for choosing me to walk this life road with you. It's the best time I've ever had.

Acknowledgments

I couldn't have walked this journey of healing without the support of family and friends holding me up when my legs were a bit too wobbly to stand.

Thank you, Mom and Dad, for your unconditional love through my crashes and burns, ridiculous escapades, impromptu travels, and mountaintop victories. I wouldn't be the woman I've become without your support, your example, and your constant prayer.

Graham and Theresa Cooke, I sure enjoy being your fourth daughter. Thank you for teaching me how to rest in the truth.

I'm eternally grateful for my best friend, Kelly, who saw my bad character and chose to love me out of it, and to my beautiful Antonia, who believed in me when I didn't have the strength to believe in myself. Thank you for helping me make the kind of music I adore.

And then we have the Michael W. Smith family, who adopted me in all of my craziness. You took me into your home and your hearts and provided me with much more than a gig for over ten years. You gave me a family.

I still smile when thinking about the divine setup of running into Miss Andrea Lucado on the lido deck of that cruise ship. This book wouldn't be what it is without your mad editing skills. And to the best sister-in-law a girl could ever ask for, Libby Gifford. Your brilliant illustrations brought my words to life.

Thank you, Paul Young and family, for investing in our lives, for restoring our sight, and for teaching us about Papa. You truly know and extend the tangible reality of unconditional love, grace, and generosity.

Thank you, Bill Johnson and Bethel Church, for providing us with a home for years before we ever moved to Redding, California. The atmosphere and open heaven in your church and city provided the perfect place for these pages to unfold.

I adore you, Jana Burson. I knew I was going to work with you the second I met you at the FaithWords office. Thank you for being as passionate about this project as I am, and for making sure it found the perfect home with Hachette. And thank you, Duane Ward at Premiere Speakers/Premiere Authors, for believing in me. A girl never felt so special. Introducing me to Frank Breeden was a perfect fit. Working with you, Frank, as a literary agent has made the entire process a painless adventure. I've been in the safest hands.

And finally, to my dearest fans. It began with a Jonas Brothers world tour, a daily blog, and several thousands of emails asking me to write this book. Without your persistence, this project would have never happened, which is why these pages are for you.

Contents

War for Peace

When my husband, Lucas, and I self-published the first edition of *God Loves Ugly* at the end of 2010, neither of us had a clue what we were doing. I knew the music industry pretty well from being a touring musician and songwriter for ten years, but the book world was foreign terrain that seemed to have no map. We Googled a lot, blindly traipsed through uncharted waters, and hoped for the best as we shipped my first "child" all over the world from our two-man bedroom operation.

The results were overwhelming. And humbling.

The most frequent comment I received from readers was, "I started your book and read it all in one sitting." While this is, hands down, the greatest compliment any author could ever desire for his or her work, I know from personal experience that permanent freedom doesn't come quite that easily. There's no magic pill or microwavable shortcut that zaps us into our desired perfection. Freedom must be contended for carefully and very intentionally. I've lost track of the number of times I've read a life-changing book, only to find myself at a loss for words about its profound content a year later.

Why does this happen to so many of us? Why do we get excited to uncover breakthrough truth and then sit by helplessly as old patterns of destruction creep in and overtake us again? Why do the things we hate about ourselves seem to be the hardest things to change?

Hearing truth only turns the lightbulb on. Fighting for truth keeps the path lit, which is the only way to learn to walk without stumbling. If the fresh revelation that you uncover while reading this book isn't applied to your heart, unfortunately, your life will stay the same.

And that, dear friend, is not what you deserve.

As you read these pages, let me propose a challenge. Read at your own pace, some of you chewing on the words slowly, and some gulping down entire chapters with lightning speed. If you happen to be one of the read-it-all-in-one-sitting types I'm describing, I encourage you to go for it. Devour it. Plow through the book with a thirst for revelation and freedom. But as your eyes read the last page, understand that you have not reached the end. In fact, your journey is just beginning.

Go back to the "Your Turn" sections at the end of each chapter, slowly and delicately taking the time to reveal places of your heart that might be difficult to uncover. When I ask you to declare and speak truth aloud for forty days, it's because I've done it and it works. When I ask you to forgive yourself, it's because it's the only way to break the chains and move forward. Fight for your future. Fight for your healing. Lasting change will come only when you face the ugly monsters from your past, pull out the thorny lies, and replace them with the restoring balm of truth.

One day, one memory, and one moment at a time.

It takes hard work, but it's good work. It's work that, if done diligently, can alter the pages of your future, making freedom a daily reality—one that I'm truly living.

You were born for freedom. You were made for it.

And it's within your reach.

Now, let's get to work.

XOXO, Christa

GOD
LOVES
UGLY

AUGUST 1999

I picked up the phone, reluctantly dialing the only number I knew to call, the only place I was ashamed to call. Home.

My body had finally stopped listening to my slave-driving head. I'd drained my precious reserve of performance fuel and found myself void of any desire or ability to get up from an uncomfortable college mattress that had turned into quicksand.

I had finally done it—I had reached the end of me. I cleared my throat, attempting to steady the obvious shake behind each word, but my usual strong voice had disintegrated into a hollow shell of itself.

There would be no faking it today. "Hey, Daddy, it's me."

"Christa?" I felt his immediate fatherly concern. "What's wrong, honey? Are you okay?"

I hesitated for a brief moment, knowing that once the words I feared most came out of my mouth, I could never, ever take them back. They would uncover the one thing I had spent my entire life working overtime to conceal.

I am a failure.

I let out a long, painful sigh. "Dad, I don't think I have the guts to kill myself, but, uh, I need help." My voice trailed off into nothing more than a whisper. "I'm afraid I just don't have the strength to live anymore."

IS YOUR LOVE BUCKET EMPTY?

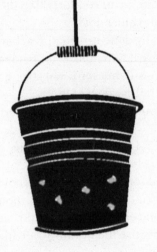

I'm Still Here
By Christa Black

The storm, the wind, the rain have met me once again
And interrupted blue
The sky turned gray, turned cold, turned winter once again
And interrupted blue

But I'm here for now
Yes, I'm here

Though storm, though wind, though rain have met me once again
And interrupted blue

I'm still here

Chapter 1

The Love Bucket

Ten Years Later

The roar of the crowd was deafening.

Well, maybe it wasn't really a roar. It was more like the ear-bleeding, nails-on-a-chalkboard sound of tires screeching in a high-pitched NASCAR peel-out. I'd never heard anything like it in my life. It was like having to lean into a wind that wasn't there, as if the sound had fists that kept punching me in the chest as I waited in the dark wings of the outdoor stage. I peered out at the fifty thousand teenagers completely out of their minds in expectation of the vision they were about to behold, said a couple of silent prayers, and prepared to walk out in front of them wearing the shortest miniskirt I'd worn in a decade.

They weren't, however, screaming for me—or my miniskirt. They were weeping, dripping snot, jumping up and down holding each other, and throwing roses, teddy bears, and sometimes bras at three gorgeous boys with flawless, curly locks of hair and faces so perfectly chiseled, they would later be cast as cherubs in a movie.

The Jonas Brothers were definitely easy on the eyes, easy on the ears, and easy for the heart, especially if you were sixteen or had a thing for dark, Italian hunky types who were raised to be perfect gentlemen.

I had been hired for their world tour after playing one

show with them at the famous Ryman Auditorium in Nashville, Tennessee. They needed a fiddle player for the gig, but I assured their manager/father when he approached me with the job that even though I was a native Texan living in country-music land, I was just a violinist who could only attempt to fake fiddle. I guess I must have been a pretty good faker, because they asked me to join their band. I have to admit, my lack of cable television left me a bit in the dark when it came to current pop culture, and I had to resort to Google to find out exactly who these teen sensations were and what all the fuss was about.

I quickly found out what the fuss was all about when I was swept up in the middle of it.

This Monterrey, Mexico, show, in front of a crowd so big it could have had its own zip code, was our first stop on a whirlwind of a world tour. The Latin fans were gushing with such admiration, zeal, and insanity, to describe them as "passionate" felt like a gross understatement. In fact, when we drove into the venue, it seemed more like we were in *Jurassic Park* than at a teenybopper concert. Each tiny, youthful body seemed to morph into Superwoman, rocking our heavy vans back and forth like teeter-totters while pounding on the thin glass barriers that separated them from their beloved obsessions.

I had always dreamed of being in the mainstream music industry. I imagined traveling the globe and filling up my passport with all sorts of colorful stamps, riding on private jets, hanging out in VIP greenrooms, laughing with Letterman and shaking hands with Conan—happily surviving on tiny amounts of sleep to dazzle and entertain millions of people. I secretly hoped for the biggest and best, the grandest and largest, the crème de la crème of tours. Well, here I was, finally sharing the stage with one of the biggest acts in the world.

As I stared out at the expectant fans in a stadium glittering with flashing cameras, a small voice inside my head whispered with pride, "Christa, you've done it, girl. You've finally made it to the big time." This had to be it. This had to be the top of the mountain. I had to have finally arrived.

We huddled, prayed, finally chanting, "Living the dream!" before running to our starting positions. Lights spun in strobe patterns, flooding the massive metal rig that held up thousands of pounds of speakers ready to challenge the screaming. LCD screens flashed and twirled with bright images and pictures, taunting the crowd to somehow reach jet-engine decibels. As I stood looking out at the blur of faces, waiting for the downbeat signaling the start of the biggest show of my life, the heart that I had expected to race with exhilaration stopped suddenly.

I swallowed hard, confused, choking back the onslaught of tears building up behind my carefully applied makeup. In the middle of what should have been my crowning moment as a musician—in the midst of the event I had practiced for my entire life in front of my bathroom mirror—an unshakable weight, as heavy as a freight train, fell on top of my heart.

I looked out at the beautiful faces of these frantic girls. They were screaming, weeping, longing for someone to love them, define them—tell them they were pretty and special. They wanted to be chosen, to have their hands touched for a brief moment, to be looked at and noticed as a treasure. I stared into the eyes of pain, of insecurity, and of questioned identity. Empathy consumed me, and familiarity reminded me of the struggles I'd fought for years to overcome. I remembered what it felt like to hurt, to feel like an alien in my own skin, to long for something more, to loathe my reflection—at one point even believing the only way out was to end my own life.

I stopped and breathed a deep sigh—the deep sigh that changed my life.

I wasn't out there for the glory I once thought I was after. I wasn't on tour in the hope of seeing my name in lights or gaining the popularity or fame I had once coveted. I wasn't hired as just another musician, playing yet another instrument and another passing song.

I was there for one thing: to become a friend, a champion, a sister, and a cheerleader for those faces in the crowd. I found myself longing to bestow love on kindred hearts navigating through waters I'd already charted, dying to know the truth that I could clearly see. They were unique, irresistibly beautiful, and powerfully important.

These new feelings were so overwhelming that, as I looked into their eyes, they were changing my heart, becoming my purpose, and completely, absolutely, undeniably taking my breath away.

IN THE BEGINNING

If *Webster's Dictionary* defined the term "Great American Family," you might just find a picture of my family beside the definition. Our checklist was more than complete:

1. Mom: Check   ✔
2. Dad: Check   ✔
3. Dog: Check   ✔
4. Food: Check   ✔
   (homemade food, at that)
5. Clothes: Check   ✔
6. House: Check   ✔
7. Car: Check   ✔
8. Middle-Class: Check   ✔
9. Easy-Bake Oven: Check   ✔
10. Disco Record Player: Check   ✔
11. Trampoline: Check, Check   ✔✔

By most textbook standards and definitely from the outside looking in, I should have had absolutely nothing to complain about. There was no obvious reason for nightmares, fears, or stumbling hesitations. But there was always one enormous problem that, as I grew older, I could never seem to sweep completely under the rug, no matter how hard I tried.

My first memory of life was sexual.

It wasn't playing out in the backyard or laughing. It wasn't learning how to take my first steps or French braiding my Cabbage Patch doll's hair. Instead of the innocence of a wide-eyed childhood, the discovery of the world with excitement and fearless courage, a few experiences within the sexual realm overshadowed and influenced the enormous wealth of good that came my way.

I'm still not exactly sure what happened—vague memories of a young man working at my mom's furniture store, fragments of being touched in a way no baby should be touched, and a sexual realm that opened up a secret place of dark shame and dirty emotions.

I felt disgusting. I felt unworthy. I felt, well—wrong. No one taught me as a three-year-old child to hide and be ashamed, but somehow I knew. The core of my humanity sensed that those feelings of sexuality were premature and that I should run and hide when "the blackness" would come rushing over me. Its talons of shame and self-hatred ran deep and hooked strong, frying my emotional circuit board like an electric power line hitting water.

Running and hiding weren't very easy inside a home supplied with unlimited amounts of unconditional love. The thing was, I had already built a castle of protection around my tiny wounded heart to cope with my experience. My parents continued their onslaught of lavish affection, unaware of the trauma I had encountered, so no matter how much love they gave, I continued to feel completely unworthy of the extravagant gift they were giving.

The truth didn't really matter. It didn't matter that my parents loved me more than life itself. It didn't matter that

I was a beautiful little girl with my whole life ahead of me, with pages of my book waiting to be written and uncharted territory explored. It didn't matter that I wasn't really tarnished. I wasn't really ruined. I wasn't really broken.

What mattered was, I believed that I was.

My worldview had been forged from a circumstance that was far outside of my control, and yet every emotion, every thought, and every action still filtered through that one distorted lens.

I saw the world, and my world was covered in a disgusting black lie.

What I believed wasn't the truth, but I still lived every moment under its power. I couldn't help it. Every move that I made, every word that came out of my mouth, the way I treated people, and the way I let them treat me were direct results of an inner list of beliefs written on the fabric of my existence.

My truth was: I'm dirty.

My truth was: I'm ugly.

My truth was: I'm unworthy of love.

So as an innocent little girl, learning the ropes of life, I did what any little girl in my position would do.

I acted out what I believed to be true.

THE LEAKY BUCKET

People cope in different ways when they believe lies about themselves. They act differently when they believe they're unwanted, rejected, or damaged—maybe believing they're dirty, wrong, or unlovable. My beliefs about myself might not have been true, but they were the most powerful things in my little universe, and I unconsciously lived through their power every single day. Some cope by giving up all hope. Some try to blend in or become invisible. Some lash out in rebellion and anger. Others become promiscuous.

Well, for whatever reason, I must have thumbed through the coping manual and decided on the overachievement/perfectionist path, dealing with inadequacy through a little thing we all know as performance.

I quickly morphed into a success addict by the ridiculously early age of three. Achieving somehow gave me a small semblance of importance and recognition that temporarily appeased the deficiency I felt within my confused heart.

School was the perfect place to overachieve. I would walk next door to my elderly neighbor's big white house, crawl up on her afghan-covered couch, and listen intently as she taught me the basics of the English language. Since I'd already learned how to read, teachers quickly advanced me from preschool to kindergarten, and I was instantly labeled a "smart kid" in the class. I loved this label—I loved any sort of attention that led to recognition—feeding my search for new ways to replicate the drugs of success and status.

Then came musical achievement, with violin lessons beginning before some kids are even potty trained. The Suzuki String Program at Texas Tech University accepted children in a wide range of ages, and I was determined to eventually be the best. We'd all pile in the concert hall wearing our matching red shirts—row after row of students of every age playing long concerts in unison as a big orchestral group. The longer the concert continued, the more advanced the pieces became. I was always the youngest kid standing as the difficulty level increased, watching my peers drop like flies around me while I stood, nose held high, to play yet another piece. I hated having to eventually sit down, admitting to an entire audience of people that I wasn't good enough to play the next song.

Failure was not an option.

I had to win every race, beat the boys at tetherball, and finish every test first with a boasting A on top. I even got detention one time for completing both my assignment and the paper for the girl sitting next to me. She always finished last. I was just trying to help.

Elementary school should have been filled with memories of playgrounds and pigtails. Instead it was a blurry race to the finish. I knew exactly how to perform my way to a quick feeling of success, but the drug would last for only a brief moment—it never seemed to be quite enough. Shame from my past always came barging right back through the door, stronger than ever, as soon as the trophy was won, the play was over, or the concerto was performed and the curtain had been drawn.

One summer Saturday afternoon, my mother and I headed up to a local nursing home to sing for a group of white-haired old ladies in need of some entertainment. We pressed play on the tape player, I proudly climbed up on a metal folding chair—my stage—and with everything I had, my five-year-old lungs belted melodies I had practiced endlessly while standing on our living room hearth. Instead of enjoying the applause that followed, I spent the rest of the week berating myself for forgetting the words to the second verse, which had resulted in a ripple of chuckles and a very loud "Aw, isn't she cute."

I didn't want to be cute. I wanted to be the best.

It didn't matter that my left brain wasn't naturally inclined toward science and math. I still had to get first place at the science fair. It didn't matter that I was long and tall, without a gymnast's physique. I practiced day in and day out in the front yard, flipping and flopping to keep up with the short girls on the block. I had no idea how to be comfortable in my own skin and with my own abilities. I needed my abilities and your abilities too, and if

I wasn't naturally good at something, I'd slave-drive myself until I was good enough.

Affirmation was my best friend, or so I thought.

Someone would praise me for a performance, but the leaky bucket of my heart seemed unable to hold on to the words. It couldn't. There seemed to be holes everywhere in my soul, spilling the one substance I desperately wanted to hold on to. I constantly needed someone to tell me that I was a success, that I was good enough, that I was the best, or even that I was just okay. But no matter how much praise I received, it was never enough to fill my deficient heart, never enough to shake the feeling that deep down, my greatest fear was true.

I was really, truly unworthy of love.

On many occasions when I was a kid behaving irrationally, my beautiful mother would bend down, look me in the eyes, and say, "Christa, is your love bucket empty, honey?" I was a walking bucket made for love, but there were massive holes torn in the bucket of my heart by the punches of my past, and the substance of love seemed to slip through me like sand through an hourglass.

The one thing I wanted was the one thing I couldn't seem to hold on to.

On top of everything, being loved continuously when you believe that you're unlovable is like throwing salt on a wound. It stings like acid. You want it desperately, instinctively knowing deep down you were wired to need it. In fact, I guarantee you even Adolf Hitler, when he was a baby, longed to be loved and held and cherished. But the more love my parents gave, the more unworthy of love I behaved, constantly trying to find ways to make up for the void and the pain that resided like a monster inside my heart.

I thought surely if they caught a glimpse of what was going on inside my head in secret places, my parents, peers, and teachers would stop their extravagant affection. That wasn't true, of course, but that didn't matter.

What mattered was, it was my truth, and I believed it more than I believed the sky was blue.

MENTAL CHAINS

As a young girl, I would spend hours getting myself ready for school, but the battle was lost before I ever stepped in front of the mirror. I would set my alarm early and spend hours washing, drying, crimping, curling, and spraying every strand of hair, always frustrated that nothing was ever good enough. I was convinced that my reflection was always going to be ugly, that ugly was all I ever saw. I might have felt better about myself some days than others, depending on how well my perm was cooperating, but ultimately, I could never win. I lived most of my childhood feeling sorry for myself, at the mercy of a body, face, and hair that existed to torment me—staring at a reflection that I despised with a vengeance.

My belief created a victim mentality.

Victims aren't just homeless people living under bridges or people surviving on food stamps. They're also upstanding citizens, successful doctors, bank presidents, and your neighbor living behind the white picket fence next door. A victim isn't just a person at the mercy of an unfortunate circumstance. A victim is a person who continues to stay in the mental chains of that circumstance long after the circumstance has gone.

Most people in this world have been victimized in one way or another. It's unavoidable in our crazy, unpredictable world. You might have been bullied and made fun of growing up, or maybe you were abused in your own home. Your boss might love to embarrass you in front of everyone, or maybe you're the outcast in your own family.

You could have been orphaned, widowed, cheated on, or abandoned.

Whatever has happened to you can never be changed. We can't reverse time, and we can't rewrite history. We can't turn back the clock or jump in a DeLorean, power up the flux capacitor, and head back in time with Marty McFly. What's done is done. That might sound a bit morbid to some, but it's the raw, unedited truth. The worst thing victims can possibly do is allow what has happened to them to dictate what is going to happen.

I was a victim of circumstances that led to limitations in my mind for most of my life, even though on the outside I was richly blessed, compared to most. But I believed in pain more than I believed in healing. I believed in what I saw more than in what I could dream. I believed in the past more than I believed in the future. I believed in my limitations more than I believed in my potential. In order to change anything, I had to change what I believed. I had to change my perspective and contend to change my mind.

You weren't born seeing the world through your personal lens. Your worldview was developed over time, cultivated, and learned from experiences, trauma, parents, siblings, teachers, and peers.

Most of our parents, teachers, and friends did the best job they could with what they had, and some of them didn't have much to begin with. They yell at you because their mothers yelled at them, or they ignore you because their fathers ignored them. They hit because they were hit. Their behavior is sometimes just a reaction to a wound that never got the chance to heal. People tend to pass along what's been passed along to them.

These hard cycles of abuse, neglect, rejection, fear, and worry have a tendency to continue their landslide of destruction by passing from mothers and fathers to daughters and sons. We learn these patterns and behavior traits from the environments we were raised in and from the things that have happened to us, and unfortunately these cycles don't just stop on their own.

They have to be stopped.

WISHING VERSUS BELIEVING

I have two close friends who grew up in terrible situations.

Mark's southern accent quickly reveals his roots, but you would never be able to tell by looking at his immaculate exterior and pearly white smile that he came from extreme poverty; verbal, physical, and sexual abuse; and a South Carolina trailer park. His dad would introduce him, at the age of three, to people as his "faggot son," beat him up, push him around, and point loaded guns at the family for sport. Mark lived on food stamps and went to bed hungry. He wore hand-me-downs and was constantly bullied. One night after a few too many beers, his dad decided to set their trailer on fire, depriving the family of their childhood pictures and keepsakes. Any time I meet a member of Mark's family (or he calls and asks me to pray because his sister is missing again, on another crystal-meth binge), I'm in complete shock. He defies all statistics, logic, and odds to have beaten down the generations of gates that held him prisoner and moved on to be extremely well spoken, loved, stable, and successful in his field. He's that one friend who is always known to bring a good, deep laugh (and a little bit of crazy fun) to any situation, always looks at the glass as half-full, and has completely dedicated his life to helping those around him who are in need, regardless of who they are and what he can get from the process. In fact, I don't think I've ever met anyone more selflessly reliable as a friend than my dearest forever-brother, Mark.

At seventeen, completely broke and with nothing to his name except a dream and some extra-strength determination, he hopped in an old car with a friend, left his past behind him, and drove over five hundred miles to Nashville, Tennessee. Now, even though his upbringing should have produced someone destined for the trailer park, he is one of the most successful, incredible, sought-after songwriters I know, jetting back and forth between his three places in New York, LA, and Nashville.

He didn't just wish for more. He determined in his heart and mind to believe that he *was* more.

My high school best friend Lacy grew up hating her family. She hated that they were all alcoholics. She hated that they were all chain-smokers. She hated that her single mother would bring drunken men home to sleep with in the room next to hers. Then she hated her new step-dad for watching and touching her in the darkness as she slept. She hated the way no one in her family had gone to college. She hated how they always lived below the middle-class line, jumping from job to job and relationship to relationship, existing in a marijuana-induced daze.

The last time I spoke with her, years ago, I was shocked and grieved to hear that everything she hated and despised about her own family, she had become. She was an alcoholic. She was a chain-smoker. She had four different locks on her front door because of the amount of drugs stashed in her tiny apartment. She was nervously laughing, trying to hide the pain, while telling me about her present situation—her live-in boyfriend had announced to her that he was gay, but they decided to save money and wait until their lease was up to part ways, ignoring each other in the meantime as they coexisted in silent pain. She had dropped out of college and was waiting tables at a local restaurant, jumping into bed with anyone who would take her, girl or boy, miserable and living in the same downward spiral she despised her family for.

We used to sit on her front porch in high school, talking about our dreams for the future. Believe me, not one of her dreams even remotely resembled the nightmare that was going on in the house behind us. She even swore over and over with violent fury that this poverty lifestyle would never be her fate. But somewhere deep inside that sixteen-year-old heart, this hard life was all she truly believed she deserved. She longed to be free from the past generations, who had written a painful, crippling history, but wishing for something and believing something are not the same thing.

Wishing for something never changes anything, but believing produces action.

And action changes everything.

MIND RENOVATION

You are a house.

You live in this house; you move in this house; you exist in this house.

The foundation of your house is your belief system, and the bricks laid are thoughts that you allow inside your head.

Some houses are strong and large. Some are beautiful and always expanding. But others are unstable and crumbling or small and falling apart. Some have pristine yards, but others look like they might be in the jungle.

The entire structure of your life is built upon what you believe, so everything that's ever happened to you has helped lay a foundation that determines the structure of your whole life. Bricks that are damaged, crumbling, or out of place compromise the entire house, just as my first memory compromised my entire belief system. The lie that I was unworthy, unlovable, tarnished, and dirty crippled me for years, even though it wasn't remotely true. The structure of my house suffered the consequences until the lies were removed.

A lot of you have beautiful houses on the outside. This

is normal in our appearance-obsessed culture. You work overtime to make sure the hedges are trimmed, the shutters are painted, and onlookers admire your immaculate appearance. You might even have a living room for entertaining or a deck for parties, where people can see just enough of the inside to think that everything is spotless, happy, and perfect. But heaven forbid your guests look in the basement. There are locks on secret vaults and forgotten dungeons inside your heart. You believe if you can keep up the perception of perfection, no one will see the shameful disasters inside.

You think that if the exterior of the house is shiny and new, constantly upgraded and improved, maybe the neighbors won't notice the stench coming from the trash piling up inside. Maybe people walking by won't be able to see the disaster zone that you'd rather not face and clean up. If you can just cover it up, why put in the sweat and tears to remove the junk?

I knew all about this way of living. It was the way I coped with pain for the majority of my life. If I could make my exterior as perfect as possible and win awards for how powerful and successful my house was, I hoped no one would ever have to see the filthy interior, with its shameful rooms, black holes, and secretive garbage. In fact, keeping myself preoccupied with the appearance of my house was an attempt to try to make up for all the problems inside. I prayed that if I just kept applying a new coat of paint, no one would find out that the plumbing was shot and that termites were eating me alive.

The problem with this approach to life is that the house of your heart can never be a home. If you have rooms inside your heart that you're ashamed of or embarrassed by or that you simply want to avoid, then you will never fully be at rest within yourself and the home of your soul. You'll never know the peace of true contentment—the deep sighs that release life.

One of the most important things I've ever done, and that you could ever do, is to begin to replace the lies, represented by the faulty bricks, one by one, with the real truth. You might have to face ugly monsters that you've fought to ignore. You might have to clean out dirty black rooms that you've been petrified to remember, but your house will never be free and whole until you do.

It's time to barge into every corridor in the house of your heart and find out if what you're allowing to live under your roof deserves to live there. You're the only landlord you're ever going to have. You're the only one who can kick out unwanted squatters. You're the only one who can give the green light to repaint, remodel, and restore. And your heart is the only home you're ever going to have any real control over.

Taking on the project of heart renovation isn't an easy task. In fact, it takes a lot of hard work. But I promise, being at peace and at rest inside your heart is worth the work. It changes everything about everything.

And it starts in the place you know all too well.

Your head.

↓ YOUR TURN:
Who Do You Think You Are?

I like lists. I make a lot of them. I'm not exceptionally organized or administrative, so making lists helps me sort the jumble in my head so that I can see it all on paper.

I want you to go somewhere quiet and turn off your cell phone and your TV. Make sure you're not going to be interrupted by homework, kids, friends, or obligations. Get out your computer, your journal, or just a piece of paper. I want you to make a very important list.

What do you really believe about yourself?

There's no detail too insignificant or too small to write down. Remember, no one is going to read this but you, so fight to be extremely, painfully honest. Write down every single thing that you believe about yourself, good or bad.

Are you caring? Are you loving? Are you untrustworthy? Are you insecure? Are you a bad friend or a good friend? Do you believe that you're ugly? Stupid? Unworthy of love? Do you believe you'll always fail? That you'll always be second best? That you'll always be alone?

What situations happened in your past that helped you come to these beliefs?

When I first made this list, I wrote down how much I hated the cellulite on the back of my butt and believed that if I ever got married, my husband would be so disappointed that he would divorce me. I thought I was going to have to back out of doorways for the rest of my life.

You'll feel silly writing some of your beliefs down, but do it anyway. You need to get them out where you can see them. You need to recognize what you believe before you can ever start changing it.

Some of you have had such grotesque tragedy occur in your lives, it makes my past trauma look like a pleasant walk through the park. And some of you feel guilty because you're still struggling with identity, but you can't pinpoint anything seemingly traumatic. Do not compare your pain. Pain is pain is pain is pain. The pain of a privileged child being shipped off to boarding school is just as crippling to that person as the pain of someone who has been orphaned, beaten, or sexually abused. Deal with *your* life and situation, and do not compare yourself to others around you. Everyone, despite the details of his or her story, has the same opportunity to find freedom. The journey will be harder for some, depending upon what they've been through, especially in the early, defining stages of life. But no one is a lost cause. No one is a hopeless case.

No one.

What thoughts consistently roll through your head?

The University of Minnesota conducted a study and found that the average person thinks fifteen hundred unconscious words per minute, and that 80 percent of those words are negative. I don't know about you, but to me that average is horrific.

I'll never forget the first time I consciously paid attention to my own thoughts, and, I have to admit, what I found was jaw dropping. Up until that point I had just accepted my thinking as gospel truth as it rolled through my brain like a ticker-tape newsreel, feeding information to every part of my body and soul. For several minutes while walking along Fourteenth Street in New York City, I allowed myself to really be conscious of what I was thinking.

I thought I was ugly that day. I thought my jeans made

my butt look big. I thought I would never have a boyfriend. I thought I could never have the apartment that I wanted. I thought my skin was embarrassingly broken out. I felt sorry for myself for being broke. I thought I was trapped and crippled by my addictions. I thought and thought, and not one thought out of hundreds was in the same galaxy as anything positive.

Pay attention to your thinking. What strolls through that brain of yours every day? What do you allow yourself to dwell on, to feed on? What consumes your mind?

Do your thoughts tend toward worry, fear, anxiety, negativity, inadequacy, or self-hatred? Do you have thoughts about how you can do anything and believe that the day holds endless possibilities for you? Do you think that you are more than enough, lovable, worthy, and amazing? Or do you have thoughts that are defeatist, crippling, or that you're damaged goods?

Write down everything that comes to mind. You need to see this list on paper and acknowledge what you're allowing to dictate the tone of your life.

Your thoughts about yourself come from the beliefs that you hold on to. Your mind doesn't come up with these things randomly—it has learned what to think from what you have experienced, helping to create your belief system. Once you start to challenge what you believe, you have to challenge what you naturally think.

Declarations

You now have two lists: (1) what you believe about yourself and (2) what thoughts you allow to consume you.

Begin to challenge your thoughts and beliefs. If you believe you're ugly but you want to change your perception, then write out a challenge to that belief in the form of a declaration. When your thoughts begin to naturally gravitate toward the negative, be ready to speak the opposite out loud. You need to actually hear yourself saying some of these statements to begin changing your head and your heart.

Let me give you an example.

"I challenge the core belief that I am _____ and do not accept it in my mind and heart anymore. I'm choosing to believe that I am _____, regardless of what I see or feel."

This life is so precious and goes by so fast. We get only one shot, one chance, and one go-around. What you believe about yourself has the ability to change everything from this point on, regardless of how old you are, how much time you think you've wasted, or how impossible you think it is to change. You can change—we all can. The power we possess is in the choice that we hold.

It's time to take a good look inside and find out if what you believe about yourself is what you should believe about yourself.

It's time to find out the truth.

God Loves Ugly
By Christa Black

You said that I wasn't pretty, so I just believed you
You said that I wasn't special, so I lived that way
With critical gazes and brutal amazement
At how my reflection could be so imperfect
With all of my blemishes how could somebody want me?

CHORUS:

But God loves ugly—He doesn't see the way I see
God takes ugly and turns it into something that is beautiful
Apparently I'm beautiful 'cause you love me

I've tried to clean up the outside all shiny and new
Worked overtime to thin up and look right
But inside I knew
Deep in the bottom were secrets I thought I could try to ignore
Old ghosts in my corridor never get tired of haunting the past
*   that's in me*

CHORUS:

But God loves ugly—He doesn't see the way I see
God takes ugly and turns it into something that is beautiful
Apparently I'm beautiful 'cause you love me

BRIDGE:

Help me believe why you love me when I know you see
You see everything
Help me believe why you love me when I know you see inside and
*   you still say*
I'm beautiful
You're telling me I'm beautiful
You're screaming out, so beautiful
And I'm finding out I'm beautiful
You're making me so beautiful
Now I can see I'm beautiful
'Cause you love me

Chapter 2

Sticks and Stones

My parents were determined that my little brother, Michael, and I would have the best education possible, so with a little help from the grandparents and forsaking new clothes and upgraded cars, they scraped and saved their few pennies to send us to the best private school in our West Texas town.

Since the money didn't flow like milk and honey, we rolled up to private school that first day in Dad's rust-colored hatchback, right alongside my classmates, who were getting out of shiny new Cadillacs and BMWs. I could tell this was going to be a daily reminder that I was most definitely at a disadvantage in this economically segregated world, but I had already devised a strategy to make up for this obvious strike against me.

I found that in order to be seen as someone important by the cool kids, I had to stomp on the weak. This seemed like a surefire way to land closer to the top of the food chain. Since I was miserable with myself and my leaky bucket of a heart was still unable to stay filled, I had to find something to fill it with. If I could point out someone else's low point, aiming all my cruelty at the vulnerable, maybe I could divert the masses from noticing the lovely "L-O-S-E-R" stamped across my own forehead.

My first day of fourth grade was about as exciting as Christmas Eve. Brand-new school, brand-new year—a chance to re-create myself and find a way to get in good with the popular crowd. I woke up before my alarm, took out my rows of uncomfortable pink rollers, proudly put on my ugly navy-and-white-checkered uniform as if it was a ball gown, and headed out to start all over again. I was actually excited about the uniform situation. It finally put me on an equal level with everyone in the clothes category, which I'd never been before. My one dress was secondhand, but maybe no one would notice, and I certainly wasn't going to tell anybody.

I walked into my brand-new classroom, sat down, and surveyed the room. There were definite social categories here, and I needed to find the coolest kids and begin devising my plan to join their ranks. Before I could open my bag of tricks, my eyes crossed paths with those of the cutest boy in the class, with his shiny white-blond hair and a mischievous smile. My heart instantly sank to my stomach. It didn't flutter from an endearing wink or because he'd passed me a note divulging his undying love. To my horror, I watched as in slow motion he moved his finger up to his nose, pushing the tip upward in the shape of a pig's snout.

"Whoa, new girl," he chuckled, making sure he had an audience before completing his sentence. "You got a pig nose! Oink, oink, oink!"

All eyes slowly turned to examine the new specimen and her "pig nose," as laughs and whispers rippled through the room like a tidal wave.

If I could have, I would have melted right into the floor. I already knew I was at a disadvantage. We had less money than anyone else in my class, I was painfully aware of my strawberry blond hair, which made me stick out like a carrot in a field of lilies, and even though my grandmother called my freckles "angel kisses," I knew they weren't. They made me feel exactly like Anne Shirley felt in the *Anne of Green Gables* books. Ugly. My chances of starting out on the right foot had evaporated in front of my eyes, and no matter how hard I tried, I still couldn't fool anybody.

I was the ugly new girl, who apparently had a pig nose.

That blond-haired boy had flippantly shattered what I wanted most in this world. My deepest, most desperate, most covetous desire was to be counted among an elite crowd society refers to as "the beautiful." Attaining beauty took up the majority of my thoughts. I dreamed about how to get it, be it, conquer it, and finally attain it.

I was always told I had talent. I could sing and perform, always getting the lead role in every play and winning all my violin competitions. I was smart and bright, at the top of my class, making straight-A report cards. I was naturally athletic, getting a full volleyball scholarship to a private university. But no matter how long my list of accomplishments ran, it never seemed to be quite enough. The only thing I ever really wanted was the only thing I thought I didn't have.

Beauty.

This opinion was formulated on the sidelines of many school dances, as I watched all my friends get led out onto the floor while sitting alone, trying to act like I didn't care. It was reinforced throughout middle school as boys shamelessly vocalized their disapproval of my appearance. And it was ingrained in me countless times when good-looking, popular guys called me up, only to ask if I would put in a good word for them with my best friend.

Yes, I had good reason to believe I was ugly, with years of rejection confirming the argument.

To this day, if my skin is broken out, my jeans are too tight, or I'm cursed with a flat hair day, the automated programming inside my head can have a tendency to wage World War III against my emotions. Before I know it, thirty minutes in front of my own reflection has dictated the tone and mood of my entire day. It's funny how something as seemingly innocuous as a little mirror can hold such mighty power.

Many of us are familiar with the routine of standing

in front of our reflection after getting out of the shower, unsatisfied with what we see staring back at us. I've found this to be the number one demon I've faced almost every single morning for years. I trained myself to devour what I saw, screaming at the imperfections with loud machine-gun thoughts, then basing the majority of my emotions on what I'd seen.

If I had been successful at working out for the week, restricting myself enough to drop a dress size, or avoiding the donut box on the counter, I might feel a semblance of peace as I walked out the door. However, if I had a muffin-top waistline gushing over the brim of my jeans and didn't have a long top to cover up the mess I'd made, or if my flat hair refused to cooperate with my arsenal of hair products, the day seemed to be shot before I had a chance to even start it.

UNATTAINABLE

I was finally hitting teenager status when my daddy was offered the senior pastor position of a bigger Texas church, so we packed up the moving van and headed to Abilene. I was excited about my first public school experience, but it still felt like I was walking into a lion's den of hungry cubs ready to devour fresh, new meat. I knew one girl from a gymnastics class I'd taken that summer, but she definitely didn't need any more friends, being one of the most popular girls in our grade. I was really going to have to pour on the charm (or the slime, whichever was needed) to find my place in one of the scariest, most frightening, most segregated places on the planet: the school cafeteria.

I weaseled my way into a seat at the popular table with funny stories and information I'd gathered about easy targets. If I could make someone laugh at the expense of someone else, I knew I could earn a place as the court jester. It had always worked in the past. I wasn't in the popular crowd because I was rich like some, or exceptionally good-looking like others, or because I needed a trainer bra like the rare handful of girls at age twelve. I had to work an angle to get in there, and I knew I could lose that angle just as fast as I had found it. I never achieved my permanent seat on the popular platform. I was always on the outskirts, doing whatever I needed to maintain my golden ticket to the cool crowd.

This particular lunchtime, Veronica (one of the ten girls who actually needed that trainer bra) had just broken up with John, and I smelled my chance at love. I'd had a pretty big crush on John for a while, so I sent a couple of my friends over to check out his newly single situation. If I was lucky, I might obtain the holy grail of middle school life: He might actually "go" with me. To this day I still have no idea where you were supposed to "go," especially since my transportation consisted of a skateboard I'd saved up for all summer and a pink ten-speed.

My friends came back from the boys' table to let me know he thought I was "really sweet, but he had just gotten out of a relationship and wasn't looking for anything to jump into right now."

I was kind of sad, but not crushed. That made sense in my twelve-year-old brain. Maybe in a few weeks after his heart had healed from the perilous wounds of adolescent heartbreak, I could nurse him back to health by passing love notes and slow dancing with him at school functions to my favorite Boyz II Men song. A girl could dream.

The same friends I had sent out on my reconnaissance mission walked back up to me several minutes later with awkward looks on their pubescent faces. I knew this wasn't going to be good.

"Um, we know it's wrong to lie, Christa, and we've lied to you." I prepared for the blast. "John actually said he thinks you're an ugly dog and neither he, nor any of his friends, would ever 'go' with you."

At that very moment, my entire core belief system shifted. Their words ran over me like green slime from the *Ghostbusters* movie I'd watched the week before, and I can still tell you the way the air smelled, what I was wearing, and where I was standing outside of the cafeteria—praying no one had heard the sound of my heart shattering into a million pieces.

What that boy said about me became my law, my Bible, my governmental truth—my identity written on the core of my existence.

"I am a dog, and neither he nor any of his friends would ever want me. I am a dog, plain and simple. And I am unwanted."

Once again, my deepest fears were confirmed: I was still unlovable. The most popular boy in the school had said it, so it must be true. And because I chose to take his youthful words and write them on the tablet of my heart, I lived under the power of those words for the majority of my life.

I ran to the mirror in the gym locker room, staring at my tearstained face. I hadn't had time to fix my bangs that morning—was that it? Still had my pig snout; maybe that was it? Or could it be because of my flat-chest problem? I mean, someone had chanted earlier that week, "Roses are red, coal is black, why is your chest as flat as my back?" Could that be the reason he didn't want me?

Whatever it was, it took me out. It didn't mean I stopped longing to be beautiful with every fiber of my being. Some people give up when they believe something is truly unattainable, but I was exactly the opposite. I tried even harder, worked longer, and stressed deeper over my dilemma. More than anything else in the entire world, I wanted what I believed I didn't have.

For years I dedicated my mind, my emotions, and my time to looking into every mirror and window reflection and completely tearing myself apart. I would demolish what I saw, my eyes instantly ignoring the huge positives that I was blessed with to focus on the few things that I found so horrendous, I couldn't believe people didn't throw tomatoes at me when I walked by.

I've always hated the phrase "Sticks and stones may break my bones, but words will never hurt me." What a load of total garbage.

Words create. They can be the most powerful things in the world, motivating one group to hate another for nothing more than skin color or religion, or convincing thousands to follow charismatic leaders to their death by drinking poisonous punch. Words can move people to anger and violence or to love and peace.

At that life-altering moment in front of that mirror, I had the choice to reject the power of that boy's words. I didn't have to believe him. I didn't have to give his young, sixth-grade opinion that power over me, but I did, then and for years to come. I believed the words he had spoken about me and added them brick by brick to the foundation of my house, punching yet another hole in my heart-shaped bucket.

The arrows of violent words can penetrate our hearts, cutting and tearing the flesh of our souls. When we're hit by someone's words and don't understand how to remove the arrows, we become walking pincushions. I walked through life with word daggers sticking out of my back and arrows protruding from my chest. When the arrows or knives aren't removed, the flesh will try to heal around the foreign object, eventually making it a part of the soul. Every wounding word I carried slowly became a part of me. I might have stopped gushing blood after a while, but I was never able to be whole with the knives still inside.

They had to be taken out and removed in order for me to heal. I'm pretty confident that if you're living around people, you might be carrying around a few word daggers of your own. They're impossible to avoid.

Wounded people wound people.

Words continued their bloody onslaught throughout my high school years.

The bell rang, signaling the end of yet another sophomore day, and my best friend, Lacy, and I took off to the student parking lot. We were intercepted by Devon (killer athlete and one of the few African American guys in our West Texas school), and I ventured a couple of steps ahead of the two of them to give Lacy a chance to flirt properly.

"Girl," he shouted out to me after stopping his conversation with Lacy midsentence. "I never realized it before, but you got a *big butt*." He topped it off with a seductive, "Mmmmmm-hmmmmmm."

Now, let me paint a picture for you. I was a walking rail. I was five eleven, a size four; I had anything but a big backside; it was nothing to write home about. I know now that this was my good friend Devon's way of telling me he thought I was attractive, but my warped, sixteen-year-old, magazine-influenced brain translated his comment into the word "fat." From that moment on, the first thing I turned to examine in any mirror was my backside—worrying, fretting, and biting my fingernails over the fact that my butt was gargantuan and I probably cracked pavement when I walked.

We all see ourselves through a personal lens, and that lens formed a list of beliefs that had a lot of help being compiled. If you accepted every word spoken to you over the years, then your list of beliefs might have a few items on it that aren't true.

If you chose to believe your teachers when they called you stupid, then "stupid" made the list. If you chose to believe the class hunk when he called you ugly, then "ugly" made the list. If you chose to believe your mother when she said you were unwanted, then "unwanted" made the list. If you chose to believe you were rejected when you didn't get asked to prom, then "rejected" made the list. "Unlovable" might have jumped on there as well.

Experiences have the power to define you, along with words spoken within those experiences. Because of the weight I'd given to certain words spoken about me, for most of my life my concrete list looked something like this:

- I'm too ugly to ever have the boyfriend I want.
- I'm unlovable even if I get a boyfriend. He'll find out soon enough and dump me anyway.
- I'm rejected and unwanted by the people I want to want me.
- I'm completely screwed up emotionally.
- I'm always on the outskirts of where I want to be.
- I'm unable to control my body and the size and appearance of it. (And I have a huge butt, a pig nose, a flat chest, and an ugly face.)
- I'm insecure to the point of either crying all the time when I'm alone or hardening my heart and becoming cold.
- No matter what good happens to me, it will never last because I'll screw it up.
- I need to perform and be the best to be accepted.
- Beauty equals love, and I can never be beautiful enough to be loved the way I want to be, so I need to find ways to make up for my deficiency.

This is the short version. The real one went on and on and was carved in stone. I believed these things as much as I believed I was an American.

Once you choose to take other people's words and adopt them as your own, you begin to live through the power of those words. Because I chose to believe I was unwanted, unlovable, rejected, a dog, ugly, and disgusting, I approached every person I met behaving as if I was a dog.

I would walk up to a boy or a new group of people and expect them to reject me, expect the boy not to want me, expect my fate to be sealed before one word had come out of my mouth. You can imagine what happened in my life over and over again.

I became a self-fulfilling prophecy.

Because I believed with all of my heart that I was going to be rejected, I was rejected, time and time again.

My laugh got annoyingly louder when I got around a guy I was trying to impress. My mouth would babble incessantly, spilling anything and everything I could think of to make him look my way. I would find ways to brag about my achievements or talk about people I knew who might seem cool. If that didn't work, I'd try the performance angle. Maybe if he could just hear me sing he'd like me, or if I could get in as his close friend it might turn into something more.

None of my attempts ever worked. They didn't work because I was behaving as someone who was already rejected—living rejected, acting rejected, talking rejected—hoping to be loved.

If I couldn't see the value in myself, how in the world was anyone else going to see the value in me?

WATER

A good friend handed me a book several years back called *The Hidden Messages in Water.* A Japanese scientist named Masaru Emoto took high-power photos of the molecular content of water in different settings, photographing the way water reacted when exposed to certain environmental conditions: pollution, music, words, and sounds. When the words "You make me sick. I will kill you" were spoken into water or typed out and taped on the side of a glass of water, the molecules responded with disgust—sharp, harsh, jagged figures were photographed time and time again. On the other side of the spectrum, every time the words "love and appreciation" were released into the water, the pictures taken were of beautiful crystalline shapes that graced the water.

If every human is made up of 70 percent water, and the molecular structure of water responds to words, thoughts, ideas, and music, then what do you think your physical body has to endure every time you look in the mirror and either speak or think "I hate myself"? What is created in your chemical makeup every time you hear that you are ugly, disgusting, stupid, hated, or far, far worse?

Words are some of the most powerful things in the world. They can create insecurity or security. They can create the motivation to change or the discouragement to stay the same. They can create whole people, or they can destroy lives. What has negatively been spoken about you, then believed, then spoken by you continues the poisonous devastation. This destruction will continue until you finally get fed up, choose to stop the cycle, and fight the negative with every ounce of your being.

↓ YOUR TURN:
Word Daggers

Split a piece of paper in half and write "Positive" on the top of one side of the page and "Negative" on the top of the other side. Write down the main words said to you or spoken about you that helped you formulate the beliefs from your first list in Chapter 1.

What words have been spoken to you?

What did your father say about you or to you? What did your mother say? What did teachers, peers, coaches, enemies, or siblings say?

Write down everything that comes to mind, no matter how big or small, or how positive or negative it seems. If you're anything like me, the negative side will be much longer than the positive side. It certainly was when I first made my list. It wasn't that there was more negative that had been said; it was that the negative was what I tended to remember.

It's amazing how the negative can stick out. If you're living with the wounds created by word daggers over the years, negative words need to be taken out and replaced before you can ever start living out from under their power.

What words do you speak about yourself?

Your words have power. They have the power to create life or death, especially in your own life. Do you casually mention that you're stupid when you do something wrong? Do you call yourself an idiot when you make a wrong turn? Do you say things like, "Oh, that could never happen to me," or "I could never do that"? When looking in the mirror do you say things like, "I look terrible today," or "I look so fat," or "I hate my body"? Do you find yourself agreeing with the circumstance in front of you instead of getting fed up and declaring change?

So what if you seem to be clumsy? Get tired of the cycle and start declaring the opposite. So what if you never seem to get out of the pit? Get angry at your circumstance and start speaking about overcoming. Change your speech. Your body, soul, and spirit listen to every word that's spoken to them, by you and by others, and most of the time, they become what they hear.

If a family member, a boyfriend, a boss, or a friend is constantly saying terrible things to you, either remove yourself from that circumstance or, if you can't remove yourself, begin to fight those words with passionate intentionality.

Write down the opposite of every negative on your list and tape the list of positives on your mirror. Begin to speak out these positives to yourself for forty days.

Every morning when you wake up, I want you to look deep into your own eyes and audibly declare these positives to yourself. You'll feel like an impostor at first. Believe me, I know. In fact, you might really be a bad friend, a dishonest employee, a cheating wife, a loose cannon, a drug addict, a liar, or a number of other things you wish weren't true. But just because those traits have been true in your past doesn't mean they have to be the reality of your future. Sometimes just speaking the opposite begins the process of change. The more your mind, your heart, your body, your soul, and your spirit begin to hear the words come from your mouth, the more they will come into alignment with them.

You can use this as a template:

"I do not receive the words that I am _____. I replace those words of death with words of life and believe and declare that I am _____."

The only way to replace the lies with the truth is to bring those lies into the light and acknowledge them first.

Some of you are thinking to yourself, "How do you know my mother calling me stupid and ugly isn't true?" Here's a personal test that I use toward every belief system in my life. If your "truths" are leading to death in any way, shape, form, or fashion, then more than likely, they're not the truth. By death, I mean they produce things like insecurity, depression, self-hatred, fear, worry, or any other negative result. These terrible words might appear to be true, but they're not the truth of destiny over your life. There's sometimes a difference between what is true and what is truth. If your "truths" are leading to life (such as security, freedom, hope, joy, love), then they're yours to take hold of and walk into. If what is true is leading to death, then change it.

For instance, when I met my husband, one of the first things he said to me was, "Just letting you know, I'm really accident-prone." He even had a list of stories to back up his statement, from being hit by a Ford F-150 going fifty miles an hour to almost chopping off his toe with the lawnmower. The first thing I said to him was, "Well, sounds like you're going to continue to be accident-prone because you're declaring and believing that's your fate. Why don't you start declaring and believing the opposite and see what happens?"

I can't remember the last time my husband had an accident. They literally stopped. He fought to change his thinking and change his speech and started speaking the opposite over his life—even before the natural world lined up with his new belief system.

The natural world followed his declarations.

Here are a few truths that I know beyond a shadow of a doubt:

- We are all unique.
- We are all talented in our own ways.
- We are all beautiful.
- We are all worthy of love.

If that's all you have to begin with, then begin there. Your head isn't going to change on its own. It has had years on end, hour after hour of thinking a certain way, so it takes a bit of time, repetition, and revelation to reprogram it. The first thing you have to do is recognize what's up there. A lot of you haven't given a second thought to your thoughts, resulting in an emotional roller-coaster ride that never ends.

It's time to get off that ride. It's time to begin challenging your thinking. And it's time to start declaring the truth.

Don't condemn yourself when you do this. Don't be ashamed. Don't be angry or upset that you're stupid enough to believe destructive words. In fact, if "stupid" is on your list, it belongs on the negative side. Don't be mad that you're not further along than you are right now. Thank yourself for finally caring enough about your future to look inside. You might not be where you want to be, but you're going to get there.

There's massive potential inside of you—inside of all of us. Sometimes it just needs to be encouraged to come out and see the world for the first time.

Though I can't change the weather,
I can change whether or not
I'm gonna smile

Black Monday
By Christa Black

I've been red
Red, hot like a fire, burning brighter like my skin out in the sun
I love how my heart beats so fast when I'm falling in love
And I've been green
Brand-new scene, just like a flower opening for the first time
My, oh, my, I think I might just have to try

So where is my rainbow with all the colors of my life
When all those dark clouds fill the sky

CHORUS:
Black Monday, you can't get me down—no, no, no
Black Monday, turn yourself around—whoa, whoa, whoa
Take away your poisoning
You won't defeat another week
'Cause I'll put up a fight
No, Black Monday, you won't get me down this time

Oh, I've been blue
Sad but true, I get in the mood to sit and watch the clouds roll by
    through the sky
Sometimes it feels so good to cry
Now, I don't mind the drama, I don't mind a little change
But I won't just stand here out in the pouring rain

CHORUS:
Black Monday, you can't get me down—no, no, no
Black Monday, turn yourself around—whoa, whoa, whoa
Take away your poisoning
You won't defeat another week
'Cause I'll put up a fight
No, Black Monday, you won't get me down this time

Chapter 3

Puddle Jumping

I got to my hotel in Washington, DC, dropped off my bags as quickly as I could, and headed out in full patriotic fashion to explore my nation's capital. I had only several hours to wander before my gig with an artist named Michael W. Smith, and I was determined to see as much as possible. So with camera in hand I headed out on foot.

I'd been to DC once before on a school trip in the eighth grade, but being the girl who wasn't allowed to watch anything but *Star Trek* and *Garfield* on television, I'd been more excited about having cable than getting a good night's sleep. I'd scooted down to the edge of my hotel bed, turned the volume down low enough not to disturb my sleeping roommates, and stayed up far past our curfew watching something I definitely wasn't allowed to watch: *The Silence of the Lambs*. As a result of my late-night antics, I'd found myself sleepwalking through our middle school's sightseeing the next day.

This time, however, I wasn't going to miss anything. I was glad to be heading out alone, exploring at my own pace without being tied to a big group or a fact-jabbering tour guide. I strolled across the grassy mall, sat by the beautifully serene fountain in front of the Washington Monument, and stood in front of a stoic stone Lincoln while filling up my camera with every angle possible. Agenda-free meandering finally led me to the front of the Jefferson Memorial, all the while feeling wildly patriotic, as lyrics to the chorus "I'm proud to be an American" paraded through my head.

In an instant, menacing clouds eclipsed the clear sky, thunder clapped, and I turned around just in time to see huge sheets of rain begin to pound the hot summer streets. The storm hit so suddenly that there were no vendors ready to exploit tourists with ridiculously priced umbrellas. At that point, I would have been grateful for them and paid just about anything.

I stood there for five...ten...fifteen minutes watching the blackness pour, but unfortunately, the sky didn't look like it was going to let up anytime soon. The more the rain came down to cool off the earth, the more my blood began to boil.

"I just washed my hair this morning. I don't have time to wash it again before I have to play my show! My clothes, my shoes, my purse—everything is going to get completely soaked if I walk outside to even try to hail a cab! Good grief! I don't have time for this, much less want to deal with the inconvenience. Doesn't the rain know better? How dare the rain drop in and ruin my perfect sightseeing day!"

I brooded in self-pity for a good while, feeling sorry for myself at the hands of this annoying predicament that had plowed in and demolished my plans. Annoyance rapidly turned to anger, and since I didn't know exactly who or what to get mad at, I got mad at everything: the rain, Washington, me for being so stupid and forgetting to check the weather, the nonexistent umbrella salesmen, my shoes for not being waterproof, and, of course, the hotel for being so far away. If you had walked by and smiled at me, I would have been mad at you for being happy in the midst of my misery.

In some situations anger can be justified, but in others, it does nothing but ruin the moment you are in and everything around you. This nasty type of anger can be a poison that consumes everything in its path without rhyme or reason. The second I gave myself permission to surrender to its talons in capturing my mood, the feeling permeated like red dye in clear water, quickly changing the entire glassful. One part of me didn't get angry—every part of me got angry, and I saw the entire world through that fiery filter.

After several minutes of loathing, a very unexpected lightbulb went off in my head.

"Hmmm, so I'm mad at the rain, but is my anger actually doing anything to stop the rain? No. And I'm mad at myself for not checking the weather, but why would I check the weather on a perfectly clear, sunny day? I wouldn't. And I'm mad at my hotel for being far away—good grief. How ridiculous am I being right now?"

Being mad at the rain did nothing to stop the downpour. It only ruined a day that I could never get back. I realized at that moment that I always had a very clear choice: (1) I could get angry at something that was completely outside of my control and be miserable, or (2) I could accept my wet fate, throw a forced smile on my face that might turn into a real one, and go puddle jumping.

I hadn't had that much fun in a storm since I was a little girl. I'm sure the strangers who happened to catch my sideshow thought I was crazy—singing, dancing, and jumping around like an idiot. But I didn't care. I had just discovered a secret, a jewel, a treasure of the universe. I had found the power I possessed inside of myself to choose life in any situation, regardless of what my emotions were instinctively telling me to do. And let me tell you, it took an act of my will. It was anything but easy to push away anger that came so naturally and turn toward something good, but the strength and power for overcoming is inside us all, and I had just found that power.

I began to write and sing the chorus, "Black Monday, you can't get me down—no, no, no." And with every note, with every word, with every sloppy puddle jump, I got further and further away from an anger that would have ruined a day I could never get back.

EMOTIONS

I am a very emotional being. It would be safe to say that my emotions have run the majority of my life. I cry during thirty-second movie previews, shamelessly jump up and down in humiliating joy when heading backstage to meet my favorite band, and pull out my iPhone during suspenseful movies to check Wikipedia for the ending. If I let them, my emotions race up and down—good then bad, happy then sad—like a schizophrenic roller coaster with an eternal track.

Hopefully by this point in the book, you are starting to see that:

- What is done and said to you determines what you think.
- What you think helps determine what you believe.
- What you believe and think helps determine what you then feel.

THINK → BELIEVE → FEEL

For years my emotions were stronger than hurricane winds and I was at their mercy, helplessly dragged wherever they decided to pull me. The storms finally died down when I started to realize this fact.

I hold power over my emotions.

Have you ever been in traffic, somehow getting stuck behind what could possibly be the biggest idiot driver on the planet? He cuts you off, she goes too slow, or he forgets to use his blinker as he slams on the brakes to make a last-minute turn. You might scream out a few choice words, make some violent hand gestures, or race up to ride her tail.

Well, the other day, I was that idiot driver.

I wasn't really paying attention to where I was going, but when I realized I was about to miss my turn and quickly changed lanes, I cut off the small rusty brown truck behind me. I heard tires screeching in a peel-out as the wannabe race-car driver sped up beside me, only to slam on his brakes at a red light we had both unfortunately caught together. My window was open, and so was his, so I instantly got slimed with every four-letter word in the book, along with a string of insults.

I had a quick moment to decide what I was going to do. I could either match his anger and fury, which would have been extremely easy, as my temperature rose with his unnecessary rudeness, or attempt to cool the boiling blood that raced through my veins, releasing an opposing peace in the midst of his spite.

I leaned over the passenger seat, looked straight into his eyes, and with the deepest sincerity I could muster up, I yelled through my window, "Sir, I am so sorry. Please, please, forgive me. I wasn't paying attention and it was completely my fault. I promise you, the last thing I intended was to cut you off." To which I then attempted to add a little humor: "Plus, I haven't had my coffee yet this morning, and you know what a woman without her coffee can be like!"

A huge smile crossed my face as I watched his rage melt like butter on hot concrete.

I had just been a part of killing anger with kindness. I couldn't believe his reply, the opposite of the words he'd uttered not fifteen seconds before: "Aw, no harm done. I'm late for a job interview, and I'm just really nervous." He looked genuinely embarrassed and paused for a few seconds. "In fact, I'm sorry for getting so mad. I'm the one who needs to actually learn to cool down."

The entire atmosphere changed. We ended up having a friendly, unexpected conversation at the traffic light that day. I let him know I'd be praying for his job interview and wished him the best, and we both drove away smiling—kindness and peace having dispelled the destructive swords of war.

Was it my instinctive nature to match his violence word for word? You bet it was. I'm really good at insults, and my will wanted to hang out the window and punch the guy. But I chose to be an agent in helping good overcome evil, and because goodness had won, I remained at peace and brought a little peace to his day.

If good releases more good, and evil releases more evil, then what do you bring to your world?

KNOW YOUR ENEMY

Just because your emotions are inside of you doesn't mean you have to act on them, and just because you feel them doesn't mean you have to accept and obey them.

I didn't understand this concept for most of my life. When you feel insecure, you don't have to act insecure. When you feel ugly, you don't have to act ugly. When you feel like a victim, you don't have to behave like a victim. If you *are* a victim of a terrible circumstance right now, I guarantee you're disagreeing with that statement. You're thinking, "But, Christa, you don't understand what's happening to me!" You're right. I have no idea how bad your situation is at this very moment. But I do know that the first step in getting out of that situation is to invoke the power inside of you to choose to fight that hopeless thinking. Your situation might not change right away, but you will change in the middle of your situation.

Most of the time in this area of your heart, you have to go to war in order to bring peace. You have to learn to fight to bring calm into your life.

We live in such an easy, microwavable society in Western culture. When we want fast food, we can have it by the time we drive from the ordering talk box to the drive-through window. When we want a new album, we no longer have to get in our cars and drive to the store. We can go straight to iTunes and download it. (Hopefully we're all paying for music!) When we have a craving for a new outfit, iPod, or television, we can whip out our credit cards and find instant gratification, regardless of whether we have the money to pay for it. Things come so easily in our instant world that sometimes it's hard to put in the time, the will, the sweat, and the tears to fight for anything. Most people throw in the towel if they don't see immediate results or change.

Here are a few examples of situations where I know I'm probably going to have to battle emotional hurricane winds.

Feelings of Insecurity

Any time I have a flight into Los Angeles Airport, I know I'm going to battle feelings of insecurity. I've finally learned that this might not mean that I'm insecure, but it does mean I have to be prepared to fight an old enemy that I'm still seeking to permanently conquer. Big boobs with rock-hard backsides walk past me again and again, their owners carrying designer handbags, displaying sun-kissed skin, and mindlessly tossing long, flowing hair extensions to and fro. If I choose to focus on what another woman has that I don't have, I throw myself into the dungeon of jealousy. Someone else is always going to have something that you want. As perfect as some appear on the outside, no one ever has it all. If I choose, however, to look at and admire those around me, smiling and blessing the strangers I once perceived as my worst enemies, I win every time. And so do they.

You'd be surprised how powerfully disarming one woman smiling at another woman can be.

This is a huge reason why women have catty tendencies. If I walk into a room full of strangers, I always make a beeline for the women. Always. I quickly introduce myself with a smile, compliment where it's due, and dispel tensions and snotty comparisons with friendship and sincerity. Women are rude to each other because of one thing: We compare and compete. The second I let the women in the room know that I'm not a threat, that I'm an ally and I'm not at war with them, then they usually put down their defenses and aren't at war with me.

I don't believe women ever really battle each other— they're battling themselves and their own insecurities. When we finally come to realize that fact, secure in who we are and who God made us to be, I believe that women can be united like never before.

Feelings of Inadequacy

Any time I pick up a magazine, I know I'm going to have to fight feelings of inadequacy. As much as I love magazines, I have to know what I'm up against before I innocently flip through the pages.

A good warrior always knows the enemy. The "Who Wore It Better" or "Hot or Not" sections are usually the worst parts, but they're hilarious if you think about it. Basically, you're putting two of the world's most beautiful women up against each other, deciding that one of them is better than the other. The absurd reality is, both of them are breathtaking, making the rest of the world feel even worse about their present jean size and wobbly bits. If we're going to really accept that Salma Hayek loses to Kim

Kardashian in a bikini contest, then come on. The rest of us are doomed. I always wonder about the people behind the article who are deciding these beautiful women's fate. What do they look like? Who appointed them to be the glamour authorities, and why don't they ever parade in bikinis for our judgment?

I've wondered many times what it is about human nature that makes people feel better about themselves when putting others down.

I did it for years on end. I was the worst, nastiest, meanest girl in my group. But the fact was, I was swimming in feelings of inadequacy and felt the desire to constantly make fun of everyone else around me to somehow feel better about myself for a brief instant. It never lasted, of course, which was why I had to continue poking fun. Out of the overflow of the heart, the mouth speaks (Luke 6:45, NIV). A person's words will always reveal the true nature of his or her heart.

Secure people don't feel the need to demean others. They don't need to. They have succeeded in their own heads and hearts, are at peace with who they are, and want to see others succeed as well. They don't rejoice in others falling or failing—they grieve, and they offer a helping hand. They don't find happiness in the misfortunes of others—they offer a shoulder to cry on in true friendship and compassion.

Feelings of Worthlessness

Any time I find out that someone has been talking badly about me or making fun of me (either behind my back or right to my face), I know I'm going to battle feelings of worthlessness, regardless of who the person is. Does this mean that I'm worth the value of this individual's personal opinion? Absolutely not. But it does mean that I have a choice whether I'm going to accept this person's words and let the emotions that are then produced turn into worthless behavior.

I'm not referring to the wounds of a friend here. We all need people to point out our blind spots and help reveal our shortcomings. When a friend will risk my anger and pride to tell me the raw, sometimes painful truth out of love for me, I know I've found a gem. My best friend, Kelly, gave me the greatest gift I could have ever received several years ago when she braved the possibility of angry seas and confronted me on a trip to London.

Late one night she'd finally seen enough and lovingly talked to me about my need to always be the best, and about how I constantly worked to be accepted by the top, most successful, most popular people. I would overlook people who couldn't give me what I wanted, kissing butt out of insecurity and a people-pleasing mentality. Her words were hard to hear (no one ever likes to hear that they're being an idiot), but it was those words of love that helped me begin to change the areas of my heart that harbored bad character. Words of truth hurt initially, but when said out of love to make you a better person, they can prove invaluable. You might have to swallow some pride, but pride comes before the fall, and no one ever wants to fall.

I'm not talking about those words of love that might be painfully true. I'm talking about cruel, unqualified words from critical sources with malicious intentions.

I had the great privilege of having Jordin Sparks, a former American Idol and amazing friend and singer, cut one of my songs several years back. It was my first big cut as a songwriter, and I excitedly logged onto the Internet to read all the reviews the day her album dropped. Most of them were amazing, and almost all of them mentioned my controversially titled song "God Loves Ugly." But a few of them stuck out like harpoons plunging deep into my heart. Some people didn't want to hear about God, which was fine. They didn't want to hear a song that was extremely vulnerable, diving deeply away from pop fluff. I realized all too quickly that it wasn't wise or healthy for me to read these strangers' opinions. I didn't know these people. They didn't have any time or relationship invested in me. They were welcome to their thoughts, but I didn't need to hear them. Their words made me doubt who I was as a songwriter, a musician, and a person.

If you're accepting feelings of doubt, inadequacy, self-hatred, and fear produced from the opinions of critics who don't love you or want to see you become the best you can be, then you're handing over your power to someone who doesn't deserve it. I always have a choice to take someone's words, judge them against truth and love, and discard them if they don't qualify. Do I know this person and his or her values? Does this individual's opinion carry weight because it's painfully true or infuriating?

If I don't choose to weigh a critic's words against my core values, feelings of inadequacy always consume me. And let me tell you, true love never produces inadequacy and worthlessness. But if I do throw these opinions out and replace them, I can move forward to higher heights, free from fear and worry.

Feelings of Self-Hatred

Last but certainly not least, any time I look at myself in the mirror, I know I might have to battle feelings of self-hatred. It doesn't mean I don't look in the mirror, and it doesn't even mean I hate myself anymore. It just means I need to be prepared for a war that I've fought for most of my life.

When a person gets a limb amputated, phantom pains can continue for years. People will feel an itch on an arm or a leg that isn't there anymore, or pain on a part of the body that has been removed. I might have removed the lies from my life, but because they were a part of me for so long, sometimes I still have to fight the mirage. They will eventually go away, but it's a marathon to the finish—not a sprint.

If I look in the mirror and have a negative thought, producing feelings of panic that course through my entire body, I have a choice to make. I can choose to hate, to fret, to fear, to despise, to come under the feeling enough to actually become the feeling. Or I can fight to disagree. This isn't just a onetime thing. I would be lying if I said that I was perfect at the victory, but the more I consciously attack the negative, the more ground I gain.

I looked in the mirror today, and I saw roots that needed to be touched up. I saw bags under my exhausted eyes from lack of sleep. I saw stretch marks on my sides. I saw a huge red zit gracing my forehead, and naturally, I began to feel awful about myself.

And then I stopped. I chose to put on different goggles and look again, just like I did that day in Washington, DC, when I chose to take off anger and put on joy.

I saw a woman who was dedicated to seeing other women get free. I saw a passionate, determined, loyal friend. I saw a beautiful, genuine smile and an honoring wife and daughter. I saw four limbs that worked perfectly and a body that was completely whole and blessed. I saw a musician, a lover, an athlete, and a trailblazer. I saw someone who was galaxies ahead of where she used to be. I saw a woman who decided never to give up—despite the odds and the pain. I saw a woman learning how to admit when she was wrong. I saw my beautiful green eyes and adorable little nose. I saw a tall, graceful physique with long, toned arms.

I saw true beauty, both internally and externally.

In an instant, every emotion controlling me changed, my body felt calm, and my soul felt the power of peace.

You, too, have that power. You might not believe it yet, but you have it. And just like a muscle lifting weights to get stronger, your authority over your emotions will get stronger as you choose to exercise this power of choice inside of you.

THE ENEMY OF FEAR

"Come on, people. Rooooooooow!"

I'm not sure if it was the violent scream coming from behind me that made my hair stand on end or the sight of the fifteen-foot drop-off our raft was about to plunge over.

I was in the front left-hand side, my dad in the right front, my mom, brother, aunt, and uncle brought up the rear, and our fearless river guide was the rudder. He seemed to think this was all fun and games. My heart, however, took it all a bit more seriously.

Adrenaline strengthened our exhausted arms, quickening our already furious pace. Speed seemed ludicrous when we saw the rapidly approaching waterfall. Shouldn't we be backpedaling away from this monster? Before any of us had a chance to change our minds or wonder why we had voluntarily agreed to this madness, the entire raft went airborne (along with my stomach) as we flew over the edge toward the fierce waters below.

The strategy, according to our guide, was to paddle as hard as we possibly could, hitting the massive boulder at the base of the waterfall head on, somehow catapulting us through the air into safer, calmer waters. The whole plan sounded ridiculous to me, but we had passed the point of no return a few miles back.

Things didn't go according to plan. Our inexperienced paddling proved lacking as we hit the giant boulder just right of center, sending our entire raft flying sideways instead of forward down the river. In one crazy, slow-motion instant, I watched as my two-hundred-pound dad flew through the air like a rag doll at the mercy of the force, finally landing in a back bend over the side of the raft, with his head and torso flailing for air in the freezing water. His feet, however, were still caught in the boat beside me.

Our raft landed hard, racing toward a wall of rock that was impossible to avoid at that speed. The force wouldn't be an innocent bump—it would crush my dad, who was still hanging upside down in the water.

In one insane instant, I had a choice to make.

Fear was already upon me. Watching my dad helplessly bob in the water like a buoy was bad enough, but the thought of seeing him crushed in front of us was overwhelming. But fear certainly wasn't going to get the job done that day.

I took a deep breath. Dropping my oar to lean over the side of the boat, I placed my sixteen-year-old hands on his bright orange life jacket and pulled as hard as I could, knowing that his life quite possibly depended on it. Miraculously, my scrawny arms somehow lifted my father's entire body back into the boat a split second before it crashed violently into the rock.

Dad was safe, and every one of us embraced, laughed, and cried.

We found out what it meant to be grateful on the river that day, and I found out what it meant to fear.

Fear is a nasty little monster—the worst enemy of them all. Its sharp teeth scare people away from dreaming, from loving, from hoping, and eventually from even trying anymore. Fear never got me to write a book, to fall in love, or to stand up in front of a group of people and have the guts to sing my own song. I lived under fear for most of my life. Most people do to some degree. Fear might keep me from doing stupid things, like driving my car off a mountain or pointing a gun at my own head, but for the most part, it has few good qualities. If I ever give myself completely over to its blackness, I'm finished before I even start.

Fear usually keeps me from doing what I need to do. If I had come under its influence that day on the river with my family, my dad would have been crushed. Fear alerted me to the problem at hand, but if I had opened up my heart and agreed with its lies, I would have remained terrified, frozen, and immobile. Fear never saves anyone. It comes to destroy.

I was concertmaster of the Texas All-State Philharmonic Orchestra my sophomore year in high school, beating all the students from big schools with top-notch players. When it was time to try out the following year, I made up every excuse in the book not to participate. I had reached the top as a tenth grader—what if I had to take a lesser role in front of my peers whom I had led the year before? What if I couldn't maintain or surpass the mountain I had already conquered? I decided to rebel and quit instead of risking humiliation. I missed out on what could have been two more unbelievable experiences, moving me into even greater worlds as a classical violinist—all because I feared failure.

I have also feared love. My entire adolescent life, I wanted a boyfriend almost as much as I wanted beauty. I wanted to feel normal. I wanted to feel that someone, anyone, wanted me. In college certain guys did like me, but the second they got a little too close, I always reacted the same way. I would either gain ten pounds to put an actual physical layer between us, pull a one-eighty and turn cold and critical, or drop off the planet and avoid them completely. I'd scrutinize the poor guy, finding fault in everything from the way he laughed to the way he fixed his hair, just to justify my feelings, which had flipped off like a light switch overnight. I was petrified of the one thing I wanted—love. I wanted someone to love me so badly, but I was deathly afraid that if someone saw the truth inside my heart, he would run for the hills. I couldn't risk the possibility of that level of rejection, so what did I do? I rejected them first. I missed out on what could have been amazing relationships and adventures in romance because I was afraid of rejection.

Fear of being poor will prevent you from trying an occupation that you love, and fear of disappointing your parents might keep you in a college major that you absolutely hate. Fear of confrontation might make you into a doormat, and fear of being alone could hold you in an abusive relationship. Fear of dreaming will keep your life colorless, and fear of hoping will kill the life in your dreams.

Fear never likes to stand alone, either; it keeps awful company. It will plow through any open door you give it, sometimes bringing along all of its ugly friends: worry, anxiety, self-hatred, anger, depression, jealousy, rage, insecurity, and hopelessness—just to name a few of my least favorites.

I got in a fight the other day with my Studhubs (that would be husband; however, that's just too standard for creative little me), and when he brought to my attention something I had done to hurt his feelings, I blew up in defensive anger instead of humility and remorse. After a good while, my emotions finally cooled, and I was able to see that he was, in fact, right. My defensive anger was a reaction that came from fear.

Fear of inadequacy was one of my first fears in life. I hated letting people down, I hated disappointing anyone, and I definitely hated being less than perfect. I'm a work in progress, just like we all are, and I'm constantly looking at my actions and tracing them back to their roots, which were usually formed in my childhood. But my anger that day wasn't simply anger—it was rooted in and brought about by a fear of inadequacy.

THE PHYSICAL LINK

I have two good friends who had terrible stomach ulcers in the last year.

One of them just got out of a rough job situation where most of her colleagues didn't hide their dislike of her. The daily working vibe was a living hell, and she was constantly stressed-out, unable to eat or sleep well. The other friend's environment was exactly the opposite. She wasn't battling a stressful job or people who hated her—she was in a loving family, extremely privileged and well-off. You never would have known from her beautiful exterior that she was internalizing the stresses of having to navigate through murky high school waters, but she was. As a homeschooler, she would sit in her room for days at a time, barely leaving her bedroom to eat (when her stomach would allow her to), alone and isolated from the rest of her family, who wanted to help but didn't know how.

While the scenarios differed, the emotions produced were exactly the same: anxiety, fear, rejection, inadequacy, and a hint of depression hit them both, eventually bringing about the same end result in the body. Ulcers.

I know of a woman who came home as her house was being robbed. Her entry startled the thief, causing him to flee out the back window, but in his hasty exit, he was forced to leave behind several of the items he had intended to take. Fury and anger coursed through her veins at the invasion that had occurred. Hate and spite for the man who had violated her haven seethed in her body, and she was convinced that he would come back for what he had left. So she made the decision—when he returned, she was going to be ready.

For three days she sat waiting with gun in hand, boiling with anger and fury, ready to unleash revenge.

The intensity of her emotions, combined with the power of adrenaline, absolutely ruined her body.

The doctor's best explanation was "she basically fried herself." Those emotions of hate and fury essentially short-circuited her nervous system as she sat there for those three days, stewing in her rage. I'm sad to say, she now walks with a walker and is in constant pain, with a list of medical problems that didn't exist before the incident.

I'm not a scientist, and I'm definitely not a doctor, but I find it interesting that my years of acne cleared up the more I got free from feelings of self-hatred. I believe my toxic thoughts produced stress and toxins in my body, and they needed to be released somewhere. I'm not saying this is true in all cases or for all people. I understand that what we eat, genetics, and the environment are also factors. I find it humorous that my years of battling with my weight ended when I finally stopped using my mind and emotions to obsess over it; then the weight easily and naturally fell off my body. I find it interesting that I used to break out in splotchy red patches when I would get anxious or nervous, or that my head would ache when my mind would over-load with too many stressful thoughts.

I'm not saying that every illness is related to stress and emotions. I'm just saying that I believe we can't discount that the two might be linked under certain circumstances. Our bodies aren't separate from our emotions. They have to physically house the brunt of them. Have you ever thought about what years of worry physically do to your body? Or hatred? Or bitterness? Or fear?

What about the opposites? What about the power of positive thinking that produces positive emotions? What if we fought to live in the realm of our emotions with love, joy, peace, patience, kindness, goodness, faithfulness, gentleness, and self-control? What kind of physical health would those emotions produce?

POWER

You are a powerful being. You probably have no idea what power you possess inside that heart of yours. You have the power to start changing everything at this very moment—regardless of how you feel about yourself.

I hope that after reading these chapters, you're beginning your search for truth. When truth shines its light into your heart, you naturally begin to fight what you think, which then fights what you believe, which then fights what you feel.

There's no longer any need to accept every emotion you have (even if you're PMSing, ladies!). They're not to be trusted. Your emotions can be liars, especially if they've resulted from lies in your past. There's no need to be a slave to those feelings anymore. I long to be the patient, kind, humble, confident, generous person God says I am instead of the angry, impatient, fearful, insecure, and lacking person I've been. I'm learning to fight those negatives with powerful positives that can change everything. This process, however, is hard work; I have to be willing to fight my natural inclinations. Any time I see those nasty traits that come so easily for me, I have positioned myself to intentionally fight—and you can too. No matter what you've been through, or how strong your emotions are, or how impossible you feel it would be to change—you can.

I promise.

It's time to turn over a new leaf.

It's time to find out how strong you really are.

↓ YOUR TURN:
How Do You Feel?

Emotions can govern our lives, if we let them. Instead of just unconsciously having emotions and allowing their power to rule your existence, try analyzing them for a minute.

What emotions do you primarily feel?

Get extremely honest with your heart right now. Take a page or two in your journal and begin to write. There are no rules for this process. You can write just a list of words or phrases, or you can write a paragraph; maybe you want to draw a picture. Describe your feelings and emotions on that page.

Are you calm and in control, or do you feel like you're a tornado? Are you angry, jealous, insecure, fearful, loving, confident, or peaceful?

What experiences are behind the emotions?

When you get angry, what's under the anger? When you become afraid, what produces the fear? When you feel insecure, what's behind the insecurity?

Are you impatient? Impulsive? Inconsistent? Not every emotion is a bad one—only the ones that drag you down into the pit where you don't belong. Think about what brings you to that dark point—what's behind those emotions—and write that source, that instigator, beside every emotion in your life that keeps you in those perpetual cycles of destruction.

Find the correlation between the emotions you're having and what produced them in the first place.

What are you afraid of?

Fear is the most crippling emotion. It brings out the worst of the worst if you let it. It kills hope, dreams, and destiny.

What are you truly afraid of? What have you not allowed yourself to become out of fear? What are the dreams that you don't dare dream because you're afraid they're too big? What are the secret desires and passions of your heart? You weren't born fearful; you learned how to be fearful from disappointments, circumstances, and experiences. There is a reason behind every fear.

Studhubs told me the other day that he was headed out alone to hike to a waterfall deep in the woods, and I instantly burst into tears. When I got honest with myself, I realized I still carried fear from the rafting trip where my father could have easily died on the river. Once we sat down and talked, prayed, and worked through the fear and pain, I was able to let go of my anxiety and watch him go do what he loved to do—be outdoors in nature with the element of danger as a challenging friend.

What cripples you? What holds you in a cage? What dreams have you given up because you feel you're trapped, inadequate, or hopeless?

Fear will keep you away from the good in life, but you have to be honest about it before you can begin to remove it from your existence.

It's time to be free from fear. It's time to walk on water into the deep blue sea. Your greatest failure won't be your fear—your greatest failure is to allow fear to keep you from trying.

And, my dear friends, it's time to try.

every person has
a lifetime inside

The Grass Is Always Greener
By *Christa Black*

She's always wanted to sing like me
But the funny thing is that I would die to look like her
And her brother works to be like their father
A little bit braver, a little bit smarter
Just like a good boy ought to be

CHORUS:
The grass is always greener on the other side
You think that something's sweeter that you haven't even tried
And we have been so good at pulling ourselves high enough
To see over the wall
While we dream about what we've missed
We're missing out on life

There's a young girl fighting to grow up faster
While her mother hangs on to days that passed long ago
We're dropping treasure out in search for gold

BRIDGE:
I don't want to miss a thing—don't want to miss out
I forget I can sing when I don't make a sound
Don't want to miss a thing—don't want to miss out
On peace
Let me rest here knowing I can breathe
I'm breathing

She's always wanted to sing like me
But I know as hard as I try, I'll never look like her
So I'll just smile and start to sing

Chapter 4

There's Always a Reason

The neighborhood I grew up in was every kid's dream come true. The cul-de-sac at the end of the street had a community swimming pool, tennis and basketball courts, and a football field, and just about every other house on the block had kids my age. Jen was cool because her dad owned a pizza chain, and what kid doesn't want an end-less supply of pizza living three doors down? Mandy lived next door to Jen. Her dad was a state senator and she had the only two-story house on the block, giving her obvious street cred.

I spent the night down at Mandy's house one summer weekend. Her parents were out of town doing whatever state senators do, and their babysitter of choice was an older lady with massive black hair who pretty much left us alone. We could watch whatever we wanted, eyes glued to the foreign land of MTV as George Michael's tight jeans shook back and forth, raiding the cabinets of as much sugar as possible, and bossing around her little brother enough to finally make him dress up like a girl.

After wearing ourselves out with appropriate child-ish antics, we got ready for our night of endless movies by piling sleeping bags and pillows into a mountain on the couch. First movie up—the children's bedtime flick *Alien*.

Of course, I wasn't allowed to watch this (I wasn't allowed to watch *The Smurfs*), but the rebellious nature in me got as close to the TV as possible.

Now, I wasn't ridiculously rebellious at this point, just slightly mischievous. It wasn't that I didn't love and respect my parents. I just wanted to be accepted anywhere, anytime, and at any cost—more than I wanted to be obedient. And since my little love bucket craved love more than anything else, rejection at any level felt like poison to my soul. Obedience to all my parents' rules resulted in rejection from my friends, so there was no way I was going to go down that path intentionally. I was the poster child for giving in to peer pressure.

The movie ended. Mandy was fast asleep on the couch, the babysitter nowhere to be found, and in true late-night HBO fashion, boobies filled the screen. I'd never seen anything like the images that flashed in front of my eyes. I was so young, I really didn't even know anything about sex except it was a big secret and you had to kiss a lot to be good at it (or so I'd heard on the monkey bars). I had no grid for the pornography displayed, and even though I knew it was wrong, something in me kept me frozen in front of that television set. I felt an awful sense of the familiar come over me—something dark—accompanied by a shame from the past twisted with an insatiable curiosity.

The show ended, and I sat in that dark room feeling disgusting, feeling wrong, and feeling dirty. I didn't understand the spin cycle of emotions jumbling inside of my gut, but I knew it had triggered a huge monster lurking in the deep of my past.

I needed relief.

I needed comfort. I needed...

Food.

I ran to the goody cabinet in the kitchen, which was filled with all sorts of treats: Fruit Roll-Ups, cheese puffs, and Little Debbie snack cakes. I tore into a new box of

Zebra Cakes and ate two, three, shoving in four—eventually devouring all five packs. I sat there, a little girl in the darkness of the night, with an empty box and plastic wrappers littering the yellow linoleum floor. As I stuffed my face in secret, a euphoria-like control like I had never felt before comforted me. It felt incredible, like I was actually holding the reins for once in my life. It was an odd, displaced peace, but one I hoped would never go away.

To my dismay, the moment my tiny stomach couldn't take another bite, the ugly aftermath began.

"Shame on you, Christa! Shame on you for being such an idiot—for gorging your brains out! You're absolutely disgusting!" My head was well acquainted with one very loud, harsh voice.

My own.

Why had I done it? I had no idea. I had no clue what I was feeling. I was too young to make the connection between the lies that I believed and the actions that were being produced. I hated myself for what I had done, but I didn't know how not to do it. It was like a giant magnet was sucking me into that kitchen, and I was apparently made of a metal that couldn't withstand the pull.

This marked the beginning of decades haunted by a medicating food addiction.

I sat there on that cold floor, the moon shining into the room spotlighting the mess I had made, as tears began to pour out like a flash flood. I was trapped inside of myself, unable to figure out the complications of a tangled heart in constant pain from the past—too young to understand or make sense of it all.

I was a kid. I didn't know about self-hatred, let alone how to fight it. I didn't know how to replace the past lies with the truth. I did know, very clearly, that my heart was hurting, and that a hurting heart was far more painful and more confusing than anything else in the universe.

BODY, SOUL, SPIRIT

I believe that every human being on the planet is made up of three parts: body, soul, and spirit.

Your body is the suit here on earth that houses and carries out the actions and decisions of your soul. It's a follower. It will follow either your soul or your spirit—whichever one is allowed to be in control. Your soul is your mind, will, emotions, personality, and character, and your spirit is the part of you that connects with God and the spiritual realm. (We'll talk more about your spirit in the next chapter.)

Most of us are extremely aware of our bodies. We know when we're hungry, when we're tired, when we're sore from working out too much. We know what parts we're unsatisfied with after putting on our outfits for the day. We know what a headache feels like, or the physical pain of falling down and scraping a knee.

Your body is a house, and that house provides a means of carrying around the most precious cargo in the universe: you. What many of us have failed to realize, however, is that there's a massive difference and separation between the body that you live in and the soul that makes up who you really are.

We're completely obsessed with our bodies in Western culture. We diet up and down, get liposuction, nip and tuck, slave-drive our bodies into submission with exercise, get mani-pedis, shop till we drop, dye, curl, insert hair plugs, and wax.

And then there are our souls. The soul is the command center of your being. It's where you make all your decisions. It's your personality, your character, and your identity. The crazy truth is, the soul is actually more of who you are than your body. Twins can be identical on the outside, but their personalities will always be different.

They have different souls. People may initially be attracted to an exterior, but there's a personality that comes behind that physical attraction.

Your soul is made up of these three parts:

- **Your mind:** What do you think and believe about yourself, about life, about everything?
- **Your will:** What choices and decisions do you make based upon those thoughts and beliefs?
- **Your emotions:** What feelings are the results of those thoughts and beliefs?

Everything that's ever happened to you is stored in your soul whether you consciously remember it or not. It's a massive computer that takes immaculate notes. Who you are as a unique individual is recorded, making it the main-frame of your being.

Your soul is the part of you that feels the wounds of emotional pain. Any sort of pain that occurs—from something as small as falling down on the playground with no one to console you as you cry, to something as large as being hit by your father—needs to go through specific stages of healing. If it doesn't, it can become a tangled root system inside of your heart. The more those unfortunate experiences happen, the bigger the root system becomes.

Up until this point in my childhood, my soul had been carrying the heavy shame of sexual abuse, the condemnation of inadequacy, and the fear of being unloved. Was I shameful? No. Was I to blame for what had happened? No. Was I unlovable? Absolutely not. But my soul felt the sting of emotional trauma, resulting in physical actions that were carried out by my body to help appease what I was feeling inside.

I can't begin to count the times over the course of my lifetime that I've stood in the kitchen, shoveling thousands of calories of food into my mouth while bawling my eyes out. My hands felt like they were on autopilot as I violently shoved food down my throat. It always felt like something else was in control of my body—like I was a passenger on this cruel ride, at the mercy of a force that had taken over. I would cry, pray, and scream, "Why are you doing this, Christa? Why are you doing this? I hate you! Why are you doing this?" I was asking my body why it was doing something that was really a reaction to the pain in my soul.

Once again, your body is a follower. It will follow either the beating and crying or the healing and wholeness of your heart. A person addicted is never really appeasing the body—the person is always seeking to feed and tranquilize a heart and soul that are either empty or in need of relief.

When I look back on my life and find actions that are uncharacteristic of peace, security, and freedom, I can always trace those behaviors back to a wounded root. Always. It might have been as minor as being chosen last for kickball. It might have been as seemingly insignificant as going shopping and not being able to find a pair of jeans that fit right. It might have been as silly as being the only girl not asked to dance at a school function. If an event happened that produced emotional pain of any kind that didn't have a chance to heal correctly, then more than likely, the root is still there and has had a part in shaping the person I am today.

FILLERS

When things happen that cause emotional pain, it's as if a drill carves a huge hole in the bucket of our hearts. If you pour water into a bucket that has a hole in the bottom, it might not drain immediately, but it will eventually. The more holes that are drilled into our love buckets, the more we need to keep filling them up, over and over again. Sometimes we don't get the love we want or need. Sometimes it's perverted and cruel. When the bucket of our soul begins to empty, we have to fill it with something. We weren't made to be empty.

I believe that every one of us was made to run on very precious, sacred, and powerful fuel.

Love.

When we don't get the love that we need, we find counterfeits.

I remember my first unauthorized party like it was yesterday. As a freshman in high school, I had somehow won favor in the eyes of several senior girls who decided to take me under their wing and teach me their ways. I wanted to believe the morals and truths inside of me that I had been taught from an early age, but I wanted to be loved and accepted much more than I wanted to be virtuous. (Remember, rejection at any level felt like death, so I did anything and everything to avoid being rejected.)

I was already insecure being the only freshman at a senior party, so when my idol walked up and put a forty-four-ounce Big Gulp full of keg beer in front of me and said, "If you drink this, you'll be a woman," you better believe I drank it. The first swig tasted awful and stung as it chugged down my throat, but I wasn't about to stop. I'm not sure how feminine I looked trying to walk in a straight line that night, eventually passing out in the backseat of a car, but I completed my task: I was now, apparently, a woman.

I cried the first time another one of my older friends called to tell me she had discovered the beauty of smoking pot and asked me to get high with her the next time she came home from college. I said that I would, only to immediately hang up the phone and burst into tears. I wanted her to love and accept me more than I wanted to do what I knew was right, resulting in an avalanche of destructive behaviors—consuming anything that I could get my hands on for years.

I would do just about anything to remain popular or feel accepted by my friends. Sometimes it felt like they were all I had, so I put all my eggs into their feeble basket. The funny thing is, now that I'm able to look back at it all, they were just as lost as I was, trying to numb pain and cover up insecurity with anything that would help them escape reality. If you didn't like who you were sober, you got drunk to become an entirely different person. I hated reality because I hated myself, so in order to escape myself I partied. Hard. The problem was, the party would feel good only until the next morning, when the truth arose with the sun and Cinderella was back in her rags.

I learned very quickly that in order to keep escaping, I had to keep the party going. The holes in my heart bucket drained at a steady rate, meaning I constantly needed more to fill it up.

Alcohol turned into drugs, and drugs turned into depression. The poems I wrote in my high school creative-writing class gave brief glimpses into my cage. It was one I longed to be free from, but I had absolutely no idea where or how to begin to break out. The sun would be shining, but everything felt dark. I could feel a black cloud looming overhead, and even though I hated it, the familiarity of the darkness comforted me in a twisted way. Daily pain was what I truly believed I deserved. I hated it with every inch of my being, but it was all I believed I was worthy of. This core belief was an anchor in my heart, so any time I would try to climb out of the pit into freedom, the anchor would hold me fast to my daily hell.

If a tangible substance wasn't around to ingest, music became my preferred escape hatch. I would lock my door, light candles all over my room at night, and lie on the floor in the darkness as I bathed in music that gave expression to my pain. It felt as if I would become one with each note— burning, writhing, and feeding my anger and deep depression. I didn't listen to happy music. I wasn't happy. I didn't listen to hopeful music. I wasn't hopeful. I listened to toxins that fed the monster inside. If music was drenched in a spirit of depression, drugs, hate, or violence, I knew every word.

I identified with it as a familiar friend—as potent as a drug—that somehow comforted as it reminded me that I was not the only one feeling this way.

The problem with this solution, however, was that the music never did anything to change my situation. I listened to songs and bands that identified with where I was, not where I wanted to be. Nothing in me wanted to stay depressed, but by coming under the spirit of music drenched in depression, I remained depressed. By coming under the spirit of music drenched in suicide, I constantly thought about dying to end my agony.

I believe that music is birthed in certain environments and takes on the characteristics of those environments. Music reflects the spirit in which it was written, whether it's about sex, drugs, suicide, lust, hate, love, God, sunshine, hope, or whatever. I escaped through music that felt like a friend but in reality only handcuffed me to the hell that I hated.

My food bingeing was always lurking in the wings. I had started babysitting at a very early age to make my own money and would use that money to walk to the grocery store to buy boxes of Little Debbie snack cakes, which I hid behind the dollhouse in my bedroom. I was skin and bones, so no one saw my NFL linebacker eating routine as a problem, especially since a lot of it was done in secret. People thought it was funny that I could eat an entire large pizza, or two cheeseburgers, topped off with a half gallon of ice cream, by myself. Any time I would head to a friend's house, I'd make a beeline to the fridge to see what I could scavenge.

Despite my delinquency, I managed to remain the queen bee performer. Substance abuse usually comes with a lack of drive, but in my case, performance was just as much of a high as anything else. I was still all-state this and all-district that—graduating at the top of my class.

Whether it was food, cigarettes, performance, alcohol, or drugs, every day I would find some addiction to soothe my tattered soul. It needed constant attention and was always hungering for more appeasement. I felt ugly, so I would binge. I felt unwanted, so I would smoke pot. I felt unloved, so I would get drunk and try to make out with a random guy. The more I gave myself to these temporary lusts, the more I needed them. They were never enough to heal my broken heart; they offered only interim solutions that would leave me thirsting and writhing for another fix.

Deep down, I knew there had to be a solution. I knew there had to be more. Something inside of me never stopped fighting—never stopped hoping that freedom wasn't a far-off fantasy of delusional daydreams and fairy-tale endings. It had to be real. It had to be something I could find, and I was determined to finally find a way to heal the holes inside my heart—determined to find the solution my soul was longing for.

Peace.

There's Always a Reason

Late one night several years ago, I turned on the television and instantly found myself glued to a CNN special on child prostitution rings in Asian countries. The investigators secretly videotaped and interviewed "den mothers" who kept children hostage and sold them for sex, some as young as four years old. I watched in horror, sobbing into a blanket over the stories of these innocent children, irate with murderous thoughts toward the women who kept them captive and exploited them so perversely. The news reporter very briefly made a comment that stopped me in my tracks, however, mentioning how "most of the women who were the guardians of these little girls had once been child sex slaves themselves."

At that moment, my harsh judgment shifted.

I was judging a victim. I wanted to murder a victim of the same circumstance. Was the pimp mother to blame? Of course she was, but the stakes changed a bit when I found out that this life was all she had ever known, being brainwashed as a child victim herself. I can't imagine how numb one must become after being grotesquely abused from the ridiculously early age of four, passed along from one person to another on an hourly basis to perform perverted sexual acts. I can't begin to fathom the strength it takes to shut your heart down just to survive every painful moment of existence.

What about the violent kid down the street? It's easy to judge his behavior until you find out he learned it from his alcoholic father, whose favorite pastime is getting drunk and playing soccer with his son's head. What about the promiscuous girl you don't want to be associated with? It's easy to turn your nose up in the air until you find out she's being molested in her own home, causing her to cope with her violation, behaving in ways she never would have otherwise. What about the overachieving brownnoser at work who is always trying to outdo you and everyone around you? It's easy to loathe him until you find out he was told he'd never amount to anything by his father, forging his determination to overcome the haunting words.

There's always a reason for behavior you don't understand. There's always a story behind every homeless person you see, behind every violent act, behind every religious fanatic, behind every political and sexual orientation, even behind those pimp mothers I saw on television. There's a lifetime behind someone's actions, and yet, so many times, we find it justifiable to judge and accuse the actions we see from afar.

I do not condone these behaviors, but there is a way to

separate the person from the action. I hate rape, but how does hating the rapist change rape in our nation? There has to be a reason behind that person getting to such a brutal and violating point. I hate robbery, but I don't hate the robber. I haven't lived a life of hardship and deprivation that causes a need to steal for survival.

For every act of injustice, for every word of hate and violence, for every annoying laugh and perverted joke, for every rebellious nature and wounded cry—there is always a reason. Until we decide to look behind the action and commit to finding the root, our culture will stay the same. Until we decide to stop turning our backs on poverty in our local communities, we have no right to sit back and pass judgment on the crime in our area. Until we commit to helping the orphans, we have no right to shepherd our own children away from our perception of the destructive behaviors of others. Until we stand firm in aiding the single mothers, the wounded, the needy, and the lonely, God forbid we exclude them to pray for the health and happiness of our own families.

This all begins in one very familiar, very sacred, very important place: our own hearts.

One of the most important things I've ever done is take a good, deep, long, inquisitive look into my heart and ask, "Why?" Why am I not able to always love unconditionally? Why am I jealous of that person? Why do I get stone-cold and numb when certain people try to get too close? Why am I acting this way?

The second we believe we have arrived—we are deceived. I'll never stop growing, learning, and changing, and neither should you. We should all look at our hearts as precious works in progress and acknowledge that achieving complete healing and wholeness is a lifelong adventure. But I know from experience that we can all reach levels of total freedom and then take more ground.

My friends, it's time to take more ground.

↓ YOUR TURN:
Escape Hatches

We all have fillers.

For years, I looked at my food addiction as just that: a food addiction. I never thought about what was behind it. The more I attempted to simply change my behavior, the more frustrated and discouraged I became at my inability to find any victory or release. If the definition of insanity is repeating the same action but expecting different results, I was insane.

You might know the magnetic pull of food, or you might know the pull of something else. I had a lot of little monsters hiding in my closet, but food was always the constant "frenemy" during every changing season. Some of you check out in front of the television, watching hours of nothing to numb your brain from having to think about all your problems. I love TV. I've got all my favorite shows and watch them religiously, but when I choose to watch television to avoid or run from life, something is wrong. TV and movies do help me turn my brain off, but I don't avoid life and responsibility with them anymore. Some are obsessed with the Internet, constantly checking, updating, and tweaking their sites instead of dealing with relationships in real life. Once again, I love the Internet. I love my social-networking sites. But if I'm on those sites more than I am involved in actual human relationships, something needs to shift. Some drink, some do drugs, some cut, some gamble, some are workaholics, some work out, some have sex, some look at porn, and some do all of these things as a means of escape.

Get a piece of paper, your computer, or your journal.

What are your favorite means of escape?
What do you run to more than anything else?

You might not have anything, and that's wonderful. Don't create something that's not there, but get honest with yourself and ask the hard questions.

What in my life do I run to in order to find a quick fix and avoid what I need to face?

What are the roots behind these behaviors?

This will set you on a journey into places of your heart you've fought to ignore.

Take the first list that you compiled, your means of escape. Beside every escape mechanism, start to think about the circumstances that get you to the feelings that make you want to bolt for the door. What happens right before you run to the fridge? What emotions do you have that make you start gnawing away at your fingernails? Why do you suddenly have an overwhelming urge to masturbate, cut, escape through sex, blow up in anger, get drunk, gamble, or run to pornography? Are there certain things that trigger you, sending you into a downward spiral?

This process can be very painful. But you need to understand the "why" behind every destructive action. You need to see the reasons underneath the behavior. Once you realize it's not really about the substance, the substance loses power. Once the curtain is lifted and you see the real culprit, you can choose to begin the healing process in certain areas of your heart instead of trying to simply change the symptom.

Drinking is not your problem. Losing weight is not your problem. Sex, drugs, food, anger, gambling—they're not your problem. The root is the problem. Your behavior will change when the root is removed. I promise.

Hold on to this list. You're going to need it again at the end of the next chapter.

It's not easy to revisit places of pain and hurt. It's hard, and it takes time and effort on your part, but I promise you—freedom and peace are worth it.

And you deserve freedom and peace. You were made for it.

HE DOESN'T SEE
THE WAY I SEE

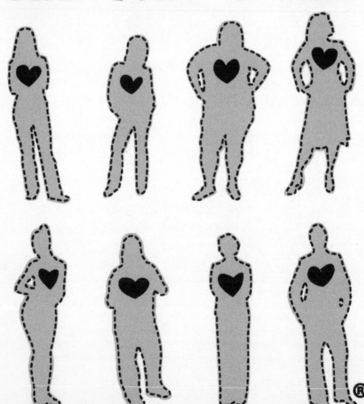

Feel So Good

By Christa Black and Josiah Bell

Now, hold on just a minute, let me understand this
There's nothing I can ever do to earn your kiss
Well, then if you say so, then I'll take them over and over again
Just kiss me over again
I'm diving in your deep end just to float down, down, down
I'm diving underneath where I can scream too loud
Funny how I have to catch my breath when you look at me that way
So look at me that way
'Cause I can't get enough of the way you love
When your love tastes so sweet

CHORUS:

'Cause you make me feel so good
Feel so good, feel so good
You make me feel so good
Feel so good, feel so good

Now, give me just a little more
I'm way too thirsty
And hold me just a little closer to your heartbeat
I think I might have found the only place that I ever want to be
Oh, how I need to be here
'Cause underneath your love I never have to run
When your love tastes so sweet

BRIDGE:

I'm diving in your deep end just to float down, down, down
I'm diving underneath so I can scream

Chapter 5

Jesus/Steve

I wish for the sake of this book, I could refer to Jesus as Steve.

Reading that line, some of you gasped in shock, shaming me for writing something so sacrilegiously absurd. Perhaps Christians misrepresenting Him for centuries is worse than wanting to call Him Steve. A few of you laughed at that name; another group of you had a very different reaction. Just seeing the word "Jesus" on the page, you got such a bad taste in your mouth, thinking of this strange guy with crazy followers, that you wanted to throw the book across the room, along with a slur of curse words, with "Jesus Christ" leading the charge. I think even He would admit, the Jesus a lot of you have experienced through some of His followers deserves to be a curse word.

His name was Murderer during the Crusades, brutally slaughtering Muslims who occupied the Holy Land. His name was Dishonest in the Middle Ages, controlling those who weren't educated enough to read his words into blind submission, poverty, and exploitive control. His name was Hate during KKK rallies, beating and lynching those with a different skin color. His name has been Condemnation outside of abortion clinics, bombing doctors to carry out His supposed violent justice. His name is still Judgment for many who stand outside of the church smoking a cigarette, or head into a bar or casino, or maybe even sell themselves on the streets.

He's been named many things by many people, but I don't believe that a lot of the things that He's remembered for in history had anything to do with the actual Jesus. In fact, I don't know one person on the entire earth who has been more misrepresented than my dear friend. If the Jesus you've met in the faces of His followers has been anything but pure, unconditional, life-changing, over-whelming buckets of lavish love and truth and grace and goodness and mercy...

You haven't met the Jesus that I have.

At first I thought I'd be covert, trying not to offend anyone. Most people, including me, have had so many terrible experiences with Christians and churches that I thought I'd just talk about God. God is ridiculously popular. Everyone usually ends up thanking Him in speeches, giving over their power to Him in AA meetings, or scream-ing out for Him when their car is about to run into a tree. I'm wild about God—over-the-moon bonkers—but if I'm going to tell you my story, I have to talk about Jesus too. I can't tell it without him. And since this is my story, and not the story of a girl raised as a Buddhist growing up in China, then I have to be honest regardless of whether or not I stay in the lines of popular opinion.

You can choose to put this book down because I said I'm into Jesus, or you can keep reading. It's a choice that is completely acceptable to make. But if you'll let me, I'd love to try to paint a different picture of my friend for you.

PK

I'm a PK, which stands for "preacher's kid." A lot of the PKs I grew up with were the worst, most rebellious, wild-est kids in the school. I'd tell people my dad was a rever-end, and they'd get this mischievous grin on their faces, as if they knew all about me from watching the crazy preacher's daughter in the movie *Footloose*. At times, her red-boot-wearing, untamed character wasn't very different from me.

I've thought a lot about why some of my PK friends and I despised the Jesus we were being spoon-fed in our homes, and I think it's probably because we got a daily, close-up look at all that's wrong with organized religion.

I believe God created the church to house a relationship with Him. The church was His idea—not man's. He wanted groups of people to come together in life, in relationships, and in love to find out how good He is, how kind and how faithful, and then to be so transformed by Him that they live every breath to overcome evil with good. Goodness should kill poverty. Goodness should adopt orphans. Goodness should see beyond color and social class. Goodness should love with the same unconditional love that we have received.

I saw churches angrily split over something as silly as the type of music being used for worship and watched my incredible dad get raked across hot coals when someone didn't like the way he did something that had nothing to do with the Bible or Jesus. I didn't really feel safe or loved by the people around me in the church setting. I saw a lot of judgment and politics that were based on performance and perfectionism, heard a lot of gossip, and felt the sting of repetitious backstabbing. What made it worse was that it was all in the name of God.

Now, the last thing I would ever want to do is dishonor my parents. They've worked their whole lives in the ministry, which isn't an easy task. They're not dealing with numbers, food, or cars—they're dealing with the hardest subjects on the planet: people. They've evolved just as we all have, with time and experience, and their journey has created two of the most incredible people I know. I have deep respect and admiration for them as parents, but even more so as powerful examples of a God who loves. They would be the first to admit that some of the things they believed and taught in the beginning are wildly different from the truth they now know, and their search has both inspired and led me into the freedom we're still learning about on a daily basis. They also realize, however, that my sharing some of our failures and successes over the years might uncover some of the lies about spirituality and are cheering me on to tell it like it is.

THE UGLY TRUTH

Church was fun when I was a kid. It meant getting candy wreaths from the white-haired ladies whose grandkids lived too far away to spoil, playing hide-and-go-seek during board meetings, and dressing up and singing "fa-la-las" during Christmas pageants. Felt boards helped tell the story of Adam and Eve and Noah's ark. We'd play Bible games to test our knowledge about what we were learning and had the chance to win money for memorizing scriptures. I won fifty dollars one time for reciting the Ten Commandments. I thought I was a millionaire.

The older I got, though, the more church lost its appeal. I had little interest in what was being preached. I was more concerned with whether or not there were any cute boys in the room and passed the Sunday morning hour with games of M.A.S.H. and tic-tac-toe scribbled on the back of my church bulletin.

The routine was always the same. Stand up, sit down, stand up again—sing an old song while an old lady played an organ, sit back down again. Don't move around. Don't speak. Don't wear hats in the building. Don't fall asleep. Don't eat anything. Dress up. And for God's sake, don't laugh and disrupt the service or you will face the wrath of twenty people and their disapproving gazes staring holes right through you. Kids seemed to be tolerated as long as they were reverent to this God that most of us didn't understand but were told to obey.

God was boring. Well, the services about Him were boring, so I just assumed He was too. I couldn't see Him, and I couldn't feel Him. He didn't seem to be cool at all, which was all I wanted to be, making it harder and harder to sit still on the pew every Sunday. He was old and ancient and didn't seem to fit in with the modern world I saw before me.

He also loved this massive list of things I couldn't do. I couldn't listen to music that didn't talk about Him. I shouldn't watch most movies. I couldn't drink, smoke, or party. I couldn't have sex. I couldn't cuss. I shouldn't wear certain things or try to be too beautiful—that was vanity and so was Barbie. I couldn't, I shouldn't, I couldn't.

This big list of "shouldn'ts and couldn'ts" needed to be followed to the letter or you'd get the look. You know the look I'm talking about—eyebrows angled into an angry slant, smirk forming on the edges of the mouth, head tilted high into the air as disapproval stares down its nose at you. I already felt terrible about myself. The last thing I needed was God and a bunch of His followers reminding me of it.

Since I couldn't see God, the only representation I had of Him were people who said they were Christians. From what I could make out, most of them were more judgmental than the rest of the world and still had all the same problems as everyone else. They still got divorced. They still went bankrupt. They still got sick and died from cancer. They still had affairs. They were still depressed— but instead of just being miserable and showing it, they had to hide the shame of their shortcomings under smiles and "amens."

If a pastor had a pornography addiction, heaven forbid he admitted it. He didn't get a slap on the wrist—he'd get a punch to the face by getting booted out of the church and losing most of his friends. If a woman was struggling with an eating disorder, she should probably hide it in order to keep her place as a Sunday school teacher. Most people worked hard to keep hidden anything that might make them look less spiritual. You drank in secret, you gambled in secret, and you definitely walked the other way if you ran into your pastor while heading into a questionable movie. Church was supposed to be a place where broken people could come and get healed and loved as they were; instead church seemed like a place where people needed to have their ducks in a row—and then to keep them in a row. If they didn't, they might tarnish their reputation and lose their leadership platform. Being counted among the spiritually mature meant you had to give a convincing performance that included a perfect facade that was humanly and spiritually impossible. It was exhausting.

The desire for perfection results in performance, while the desire for excellence is rooted in identity.

I watched as a lot of Evangelical churches warred against sin with judgmental stone throwing. They focused more on what the world had done wrong than on what God had done right. They put "bad people" under the microscope instead of magnifying the beautiful nature of a good and loving God. No wonder I didn't want to be a part of it. Who in their right mind would? The message I received in my adolescent brain was that God was moody and inconsistent and His love and affection toward me was contingent on how good I was. Well, I knew I wasn't good (I was too screwed up emotionally for that), so I did what seemed to be the only thing I could do.

I ran.

GOD LOVES UGLY

I was a senior in high school coming up on my last chance for a Babylonian drunken fest we like to call spring break when my parents informed me that I would not be accompanying my friends to the Cancún fiesta we had dreamed about for four years. Mom and Dad's nerves were overly frazzled after years of living with an angry teenager who liked to come home with the stench of cheap alcohol and cigarettes on her breath. Instead of letting me loose in Mexico, they would be taking me with them to Canada to go to the last place on earth I ever wanted to go: church.

You could smell the stench of my attitude around the house for weeks before the trip. "How dare they ruin my senior year like this! Church? Why in the world would I want to go to church?"

I hated God. Or at least I hated the God I had been presented with, and I wanted nothing to do with Him. He made me feel bad about myself all the time. To endure the shame I felt around His people, I would go to church completely high and sneak alcohol in shampoo bottles just to make it through church camp every summer.

I walked into the big, white warehouse building in Canada with my family, finally deciding on a row near the back left-hand side. This wasn't like any church I had been to before. People were raising their hands, dancing around, laughing uncontrollably—acting ridiculous, in my opinion. Of course, I was discounting all the nights I had been out of my mind at a football game or passed out on a random front lawn—ignoring the countless times I'd puked my guts out while hugging a dirty public toilet.

My arms were crossed in obvious disapproval, I refused to stand, and all I could think about was how in the world I was going to sneak away to get a much-needed cigarette.

The lady who was heading up the music that night finally put down her guitar and stopped singing. "Thank God," I thought. "It's all one step closer to being finished." To my dismay, she walked over to a violin, picked it up, and began to play.

At first, I was annoyed. Her playing meant I was further

away from any means of escape, but the more she ran
her bow back and forth over those strings, the more the
drawbridge of my heart somehow began to slowly crank
down. I had been playing the violin since I was three years
old, so the woman was speaking a language familiar to
me, one that transcended words. My ironclad defense system started to slowly retreat with every note escaping from
her beautiful instrument. It seemed like I was watching a
moment of adoration so beautiful and private, so peaceful
and serene, that I was intruding. But I longed for what she
had with every inch of my being. I felt pieces of my heart
begin to soften that had been hardened through time. I
felt the violent storm clouds begin to slowly roll away, until
suddenly, something happened that I never would have
expected in a million years.

Lightning struck. Almost literally.

One minute, I was an angry teenager addicted to anything I could get my hands on, with an intense hatred
for God, my parents, and myself, and in the next crazy,
supernatural, unexplainable instant, I was on the floor
weeping—waves of what I can only describe as electricity
pulsing through my eighteen-year-old broken frame.

To this day, I still have no idea how to rationalize what
happened to me that strange night. The logical part of
my brain laughs in disbelief, but my heart knows from the
experience that I was being loved more deeply and purely
than I had ever imagined possible. I could literally feel
the darkness peeling away—ripping from my exhausted
heart. Anger subsided under the most perfect affection
I'd ever encountered. Hatred began to tear, ever so gently, from the core of my blackened, toxic soul. I was bawling, then laughing, then resting under a river of the most
refreshing love and peace I had ever encountered.

He was real.

He was powerful.

And He was changing me in a way I had only longed for.

God wasn't just a story, a book, or a stern, robed man in the sky, scrutinizing everything I did with anger and disgust. He had become real, powerful love—the one thing I had always wanted but had never been able to find.

Love had been like a ghost. When I would finally catch up, it would slip through my fingers, only to be chased once again. For the first time in my life, I felt a love that wasn't there to haunt me. It was there to latch on and never let go.

At that moment, I knew I would never be the same. It wasn't about religion or a sterile church service. It wasn't about following rules, blind tradition, or maintaining a code of conduct. He accepted me right then at my very worst—the good, the bad, and the ugly. He loved me in the midst of my addictions, and He loved me despite my rebellion. He loved me even though I was cruel and bitter, and He loved me even though I lied and stole. He even loved me knowing I had hated Him. He knew the potential inside of me and wanted me healed. He loved the ugly parts—seeing beauty in the barren places of my life that I was ashamed of.

I had encountered a very tangible, healing, powerful being. I wasn't rationalizing Him in my head—I was experiencing Him in my heart. I couldn't deny what had happened to me, and because I really wasn't looking for it, I couldn't explain away the experience. I didn't want God; I wanted love, but apparently, the two were one and the same. It didn't make any sense in my logical brain, but I didn't care. I was different. Visibly different. No Harvard atheist could talk me out of what I had found, because I had experienced God and had been changed. He wasn't a theory or a debate.

He was a real person.

And the proof I had was a life that had been changed.

I remember returning to all my friends, excited and unashamed that I had found something better than the drugs I had been addicted to. I didn't care if they believed me or laughed at me. I had found love, and it had cast away fear. I had found a peace that had calmed the seas of my heart. I tasted a sweetness my soul had craved my entire life. There was hope, there was love, and there was freedom. I wasn't instantly zapped into perfection and wholeness—I'm still being healed and restored as we walk this journey of life together—but freedom wasn't a dream anymore. It was tangible. It was a person.

And I wanted Him more than anything else in the entire world.

RELIGION VERSUS RELATIONSHIP

I've talked to numerous people who have had encounters with the supernatural. They've told me their stories about life-altering experiences with something beyond explanation or logic. Sadly, many of them, after having those experiences, got involved with a church or a group of people who said they believed the same things but ended up crushing the life spirit of that encounter with a bunch of rules, codes, harsh words, and controlling religion.

God never wanted detached robots blindly following rules. He wanted kids to have an ongoing, interactive, life-giving relationship with Him.

In fact, I found that it was mostly people who said they were Christians who looked at me like I had a few screws loose when I would tell them about the encounter I'd had with God. Disbelief and "shame on you for exaggerating" were more than clearly written across several faces as I enthusiastically shared what had happened to my heart.

I wanted to shake them and say, "Go read your Bible and stop picking and choosing what parts are comfortable for you to believe!" Moses met God in a burning bush. Never heard anyone preach against that one. Jacob wrestled with an angel—still no fight or resistance from the church in disbelief. Paul was transformed on the road to Damascus when God showed up in a massive bright light, and as far as I was concerned (minus the bright light), the same thing had happened to me. He showed up—and I made a one-eighty.

I had met Love, and Love was good. The God I encountered was anything but safe and predictable or lethargic and boring. He was violent with love and radically fierce with forgiveness—so much so that it physically took me to my knees when I encountered Him.

New church friends informed me that I should probably break any CDs that didn't talk about Jesus. Now, I didn't want to listen to a lot of my old music—it depressed me and took me back to familiar dark places. But I couldn't figure out how in the world Celine Dion and Hootie and the Blowfish were of the devil. I broke the CDs anyway. I really wanted to get this Christian thing right, and if this was how Christians did it, then I, at least, needed to try. Every once in a while, sitting in traffic, I would cheat and listen to the secular radio station for a bit. After fifteen short minutes, shame would force my hand to reach up and turn off the pop music once again. One of my new Christian friends boasted about her abstinence from R-rated movies and how she had never laid eyes on one, nor would she ever. I sunk low in my seat, knowing I had looked at porn when I was a little kid. I was going to really have to step up my game to stay spotless in this crowd.

Often, I couldn't find scripture to support the things I was being told not to do, just a blanket statement like "You should never drink alcohol," or "You shouldn't ever have the ambition to be rich." But when I read the Bible, it said things like, "The love of money is a root of all sorts of evil" (1 Timothy 6:10). Not money itself, but the love of it. Just turning on the news was proof of this point. Wars were fought every day over people loving money, fighting for oil, land, and natural resources. As far as I could see, it actually took money to feed the poor, take care of the orphans and widows, and do all the other things we were commissioned to do. The Bible also said not to get drunk on wine, but to be filled with the Holy Spirit. (Ephesians 5:18). It never said anything about having a drink. It talked about how being filled with the Holy Spirit was way better for the soul than wine, just as I'd found that night in Canada. I had taken a drink of something that gave me a better high but didn't make me feel terrible about myself the next morning. Getting wasted was a blast sometimes, but the aftermath of regret from all the ridiculous things I had done always weighed in heavier than the initial euphoria. Most of the things I regretted in life were done when I was drunk, so this scripture made sense to me. My life was constant drama when I lived drunk in the party zone, and my life was constant peace when I would medi-tate in His presence.

The bad people at my high school sat in a certain sec-tion in the cafeteria, and most of the Christians didn't want to be associated with them for fear of looking tar-nished. By "bad" I mean they drank, slept around, and partied hard. These rebels had been my partners in crime for years. I wasn't going to abandon them just because I'd found Jesus. I didn't have the desire to go out and raise hell with them anymore, but I wasn't going to stop loving my old friends, who needed to know how worthy of love they actually were.

In fact, the more I read about this Jesus guy, the more I saw that this is what He actually did. He hung out with the most promiscuous woman in town, regardless of how onlookers misread his intentions. He really didn't care if people thought he was soliciting for sex (John 4). He always cared for people at the expense of what others thought. He invited the scum of the earth and bottom dwellers of society to dinner, even though it ruined His reputation with the pastors of his day (Luke 19). Out of compassion, He healed the lame on the Sabbath, going against strict religious law to work on their sacred day of rest (Mark 3). Status meant nothing to Him as long as He was living out the loving heart of His Father—God. In fact, the people Jesus angrily disagreed with were the religious leaders of his day, always exalting rules and law above loving those who needed to be loved.

Something never sat right inside of me with this Grand Canyon of segregation between Christians and the world. This separate and elitist attitude wasn't at all the way of the God I had encountered that night in Canada. He was so loving, so forgiving, so kind, and so gracious to me—even when I was at my worst. He never once told me to clean myself up. He even said I wasn't able to fix myself, and only He could do it for me. I felt like this new God was looking at everything I did through the judgments of His people and making lists of all the things I was doing wrong. My life didn't feel free—it felt like I was tiptoeing on eggshells and jumping through hoops.

I was listening to a CD the other day by my favorite teacher and personal friend, Graham Cooke, and with a glorious British accent (everything sounds better with a British accent) he described what he believes to be a lot of the problem with the Evangelical church in Western culture, and I wholeheartedly agree. He talked about how the biggest problem in America isn't crime or terrorism. It's not even drugs or poor education or poverty.

"The biggest problem in our world," Graham said, "is simply a lack of goodness."

In our culture, the church has a track record of focusing upon sin and judgment instead of the one thing we're supposed to rally around: a good, kind, loving, forgiving, and faithful God, who has loved us so much, we can't help but be changed by that love, and then give that love away.

As a God follower, I'm commanded to love God with

all my heart, soul, mind, and strength, and then to love my neighbor like I love myself (Luke 10:27). For years I did just that. I loved the person next to me like I loved myself, and because I consistently hated myself, I consistently hated my neighbor. Many churches and groups of God followers have exalted the logical knowledge about the love of God over the relational experience of being loved by Him on a daily basis.

But greatly loved people know how to love greatly. It wasn't until I started being loved by God (and continue to get loved every day) that I actually had an overflow of love to then give away.

I love Bono. I'm fascinated with his heart of compassion for the poor, the needy, and the broken. I believe he carries out so many things that are close to the heart of God. But reading about Bono and knowing Bono are entirely different. I can fill my head with all sorts of facts by qualified sources, watch every TV show, and read every book, but until I get around him, I will never really know what he is like.

God is the same way. It wasn't learning about Him that changed me. I knew countless Bible stories and scriptures from sitting in church services my entire life, but those facts didn't make me trust Him enough to hand over my heart. I needed an encounter with love. Meeting, feeling, and experiencing the personification of Love will change you, and after experiencing that love, all I wanted to do was be close to this God that seemed too good to be true, but actually was true.

The revelation of His unconditional love makes me run to His arms—not from them.

God doesn't make a lot of sense to my brain sometimes. The natural world makes sense because it's what I can see, but He's not natural. He's supernatural. He moves in ways and with power that defies all logic or understanding. It's why He's God and I'm not. If I was able to fix my heart and my problems, I wouldn't have needed Him, but I was desperate for something bigger than myself. I needed power. I needed powerful love. I had to have a supernatural God who was waiting to supernaturally love me into wholeness.

And that's exactly what He does, every single day, as I hand over my heart moment by moment to the safest, most loving, generous, kindest, magnificent person I've ever met.

My Father.

LOVE DEFICIENCY

Being loved by God has changed my life. Not just loving Him, but being loved by Him. In fact, 1 John 4:19 says that we love Him because He *first* loved us. I didn't know how to love God until I allowed myself to be loved by Him. How crazy is that? Because of that revelation, I've spent the last few years saying, "Okay, God, my love bucket is empty. Will you just come and love me?"

It works every time. And I've fallen deeply in love with Him in the process. I don't have to try to love God anymore. It's a natural response out of the overflow of a heart that has been greatly loved.

His love changes my pride into humility, my anger into kindness, my selfishness into generosity, and my fear into peace.

For many years I would have told you the worst problem in my life was an eating disorder or low self-esteem—addictions or depression. But I'm able to see now that those were all just symptoms of a love deficiency. I had no idea how to love myself. I wanted others to love me, to accept me, to esteem me, but I didn't love, accept, or esteem myself. In fact, I absolutely hated myself.

The reason I can't write this book without paying

homage to this magnificent God, His gentle Spirit, and my beautiful Jesus is because my experience has been that His love is actually the solution for every problem I've ever faced.

As amazing as my husband, friends, and family are, they will never be able to love me as completely and unconditionally as the God who made me. The more I allow Him to come in and love the barren parts of my heart—the broken, the abused, the shameful—the more I don't just get healed, but my life illuminates and is transformed.

Love really does conquer all.

If I'm wrong and this God stuff is all just a big, fat hoax, then you have absolutely nothing to lose.

But what if I'm right?

What if the one thing you've been missing is the love of the One who created you? What if it's the fuel that is meant to run your entire life? What if letting Him love the unlovable, shameful, hidden parts of your heart actually heals you? What if you can't do it alone—what if you need a knight in shining armor to come in and save you? And what if all you have to do is simply receive?

Don't try to clean yourself up. You can't. Don't hide your head in shame. Don't let thoughts of all the terrible things you've ever done keep you from His always open arms. Don't let the lie that you're not worthy win over the invitation that's always in front of you. Don't for one second believe that anything you've ever done has ruined you for love. It hasn't and it can't.

If God could come in and love the drugged-out, broken, abused, rebellious, hateful, angry me, He's waiting to come in and love you, whatever you've done—even if you're a murderer, a rapist, or an abuser. I know that sounds extreme, but if one sin isn't worse than another in the eyes of God, and there's an ocean of forgiveness, mercy, and love waiting for us inside His grace, we must align ourselves with this basic truth (John 1:16–17). He's not looking at the list of things you're ashamed of. He's grieved that the shameful parts of your life are keeping you away from the one thing you need: Him. He doesn't expect perfection, but through His grace, He wants to love you into healing and wholeness, giving you a purpose and a hope for the life that He created you to live.

It's never too early or too late.

Ask Him right now. Ask Him to show up and show you He's real. My beautiful friend Jess asked that very question, then walked out of her apartment, and a gust of wind blew a flyer to her chest for a Mass service that read, "Do you want to know me?—God."

Like I said, if I'm wrong, you have nothing to lose. But if I'm right, you have everything to gain.

Ask Him. Try it. I dare you.

▼ YOUR TURN:
Who Is God to You?

So up until this point, you've started thinking about these questions:

- What do you really believe about yourself?
- What words have been spoken to or about you to help form your core list of beliefs?
- What feelings are produced that consume you?
- What are your go-to coping mechanisms?
- What are the wounded roots that you see deep down in your heart?

Now it's time for my favorite list. This is a list that could be difficult for some of you because you've really never given God a second thought. Others of you have thought about it a lot, and the picture of the God I just described is galaxies away from what you've experienced from Christians or been taught in church.

Who do you believe God is?

Write down everything you can think of. Write down movie references. Write down how your earthly father skews your vision of a good and loving Heavenly Father. Where does your belief system come from? Did other people tell you what to believe? Did you come up with it on your own? Was it your experience that told you what God is really like or your lack of experience? Could you be wrong?

Write it all down. Everything.

Your picture of God will determine how you see yourself and how you see life. If you believe God is beautiful and that you're made in his image, then you will believe you're beautiful. If you believe Him when He says He's your provider, then you will live without fear of privation. If you believe nothing you ever do can separate you from His love, then you'll run to His open arms—especially when you do something you regret. If you believe that God doesn't care about you, then you will live as an orphan. If you believe that God is waiting for you to mess up and will zap you if you do, then you will live paranoid or in rebellion.

Your view of God will determine how you live.

Ask Him to show up, right here, right now.

My perspective of God was forced to shift once I'd encountered Him. I could never go back. After that experience, I finally didn't believe that He was roaming the earth prodding me with a stick every time I messed up, looking for me to fail. I finally believed what He says about Himself: that He's consumed with life because He is life. He's the author of it (Genesis 1:20–31). I found that His desire was for life and victory to be replicated in every part of my existence. This happened more and more as I encountered His love.

The thought of asking God to show up might scare some of you to death. You could be petrified of God or of the God this world has presented to you. But God says He's love, and who doesn't want an unlimited supply of unconditional love? Start right there with that one truth: Ask unconditional love to come in and love you.

But here's the catch: You must allow yourself to receive it.

He's always loved you, no matter what you've done. You're His kid. He wants to be invited in. He loves to show that He is real. He loves to cheer you on when you're down or comfort you when you cry. He loves to fill your spirit with His Spirit—loving you into wholeness. Ask this powerful, loving, safe God to surround you now. Ask Him to hold on to your heart. Ask Him to show you that He's real. Take the list you made at the end of Chapter 4 and ask Him to heal your wounded roots. Hand over your pain, your past, and your hurts—one by one. Surrender them to the only One who knows, and the only One who has the power to heal.

You might disagree with every opinion I have, and that's fine. Write it all down. It's very important.

What you believe about God, what you believe about yourself, and what thoughts and experiences you have with Him are the most important parts of the core of your existence.

These beliefs will determine how you live out every breath.

Drift Away
By Christa Black

I'm not sure where I belong
I'm not sure where I should lay my head down—lay my head down
    to sleep
I'm not sure where I fit in
I'm not sure where I should plant my feet down—plant my feet
    down
Beside Your streams of water I know I can be restored
I find it's easier to say the words than hold on to the shore

CHORUS:
I'm drifting out to where the ocean meets the sky
It's been a while since I've forgotten what it feels like not to cry
I'm needing You to help me not to drift away, drift away, drift
    away from You

I'm not sure if I can stand
I'm not sure if I can hold myself up—hold myself up anymore
It's easier to fall than to fight when your strength is failing
And my strength is failing
But I know Moses had Your help when walking through the sea
I'm needing something bigger than myself
To come and rescue me

Chapter 6

Monsters

I had made my decision: I wasn't going to plan my life around the destructive patterns of substance abuse anymore.

I knew that following my friends to big Texas universities might result in a lot of the same damaging behaviors I had leaned toward in the past, but fortunately, I'd managed to get a full volleyball scholarship to a small, private, Christian university in the middle of nowhere, Arkansas. I figured I couldn't get into too much trouble in a town of twelve thousand people where a good time meant going to the Super Walmart or throwing rocks into the river. The school appeared to be a very academic, chill environment, which felt like a huge sigh of relief for someone who had a severe case of following the crowd.

I felt like a toddler learning how to walk. I didn't want to go back to the old things that had brought me so much pain, and I knew better than to play with fire and put myself around situations that had led to my downward spiral. It wouldn't have been wrong, but it might not have been wise. I was learning to stand on new, better legs and wasn't about to take a chance that my past might creep back in and get between me and this new future I could finally see up ahead.

I'd removed myself from drugs. I wouldn't have known the first place to look for them in this tiny town where the traffic lights blinked yellow by ten p.m. I'd removed myself from alcohol. Our county was dry, and if you wanted a drink you had to drive thirty minutes just to get to the nearest bar. I'd removed myself from a partying culture. The majority of the people on campus seemed to come from perfect Christian homes with Brady Bunch families. Most seemed to wear constant smiles, the opposite sex was forbidden from the gender-segregated dorms, and cigarettes were more than frowned upon. I wondered if the people around me had ever had their noses dirty before.

But no matter how much I attempted to control my environment, how much I tried to padlock and protect my life from the pain of my past—there was just one substance that I could never, ever get away from, no matter how hard I tried.

Food.

I had been skin and bones all my life, eating whatever I wanted to self-medicate my heart without giving a second thought to my weight. But during my freshman year in college that dream metabolism began to change. I remember looking at myself naked in the mirror wondering where in the world those thighs and that butt had come from, and why they wouldn't fit into my high school jeans anymore.

Being the extremist that I am, instead of just cutting back a bit and learning how to eat correct portions, I completely freaked out and began doing the worst thing I possibly could—skipping meals. If I did eat, it was bird food: a salad without dressing here, a handful of nuts there, eventually going a day or two without anything at all but liquids. The more I deprived myself of the nutrients I required for energy, the more my cravings became like a ravenous beast that was completely out of control. The all-you-can-eat buffet in the cafeteria didn't help matters much. I'd finally go crazy from hunger and ruin my starvation stint with a ten- to fifteen-thousand-calorie binge—four entrees, three bowls of cereal, ten cookies, and a large bowl of ice cream. If the cafeteria had closed, I'd jump in the car and go from Arby's to Wendy's to Burger

King to Taco Bell, eating as I drove so I'd be ready for the next stop to repeat the binge over again.

Every single time, without fail, I'd curse and cry, yelling at myself in the rearview mirror while spouting off every name in the book. Because this behavior would be seen as weak, I made sure every bit of it remained in the dark, forcing my best smile to fool everyone around me.

Then came the shame—tsunamis of shame, beating the shore of my heart until I felt so bloody and bruised, I'd curl up in a little ball and cry my eyes out. The guilt was almost unbearable, compounded by the reality that I was struggling with something as ridiculous as food. I would fall on my face, praying for hours at a time for God to forgive me. He'd already forgiven me, but the truth was, I hadn't forgiven myself. I loved God—I really did—and I didn't want to do what I was doing, but it was beyond my control to stop myself. Somehow my performance mentality had convinced my brain that it was up to me to get my act together. I thought that in order to show God I loved Him and prove my love and devotion, I needed to fix myself. I believed that somehow the capability to clean house was within my wounded hands. (I was still walking into the revelation of God's good nature that I described at the end of the last chapter.)

I couldn't see past my past. Everything I did and said, every move I made, and every relationship I approached was filtered through the wounded lens of what had happened to me. Food had become my coping mechanism for pretty much everything: fear, apprehension, worry, nerves, anxiety, and depression. I binged before tests. I binged before the first day of school. I binged during school because I didn't know anyone to sit with in a new cafeteria filled with strange faces. I binged because no guys were looking at me. I binged because a guy was acting interested. I binged because I felt bad about bingeing. I binged for the fun of it or because I was bored. I ate to feed a deep, dark hole in my soul, but the hole was a bottomless pit that always wanted more.

My stomach would ache from being stretched beyond capacity, my body would burn, and my soul would writhe in the agony of deep self-hatred. I hated myself for doing what I was doing. I hated how weak I was. I hated not being perfect, and my reflection was a constant reminder that I didn't have it all together. My weight would yo-yo up and down, down and up. All my emotions and feelings of self-worth were dependent on whether I had been good, successful, and restrictive during a meal. If I hadn't, the pattern was always the same: out-of-control, screw-everything bingeing followed by shame and guilt for gorging; kicking myself around for a while; calling myself every name in the book inside my head and out loud to my face; repenting out of shame (and not out of a revelation of grace and love); praying desperate prayers; then swearing I'd never do it again.

The beginning of every journal entry was predictably similar. It would begin with an apology to myself or God for messing up; then I would make a vow that the next day would be different, usually with an outlined, strict workout schedule, a new eating routine, and a list of promises and rules that I swore to follow.

The entry would always look something like this:

- I will never binge like that again. Ever.
- I will get up early and work out for two hours. At least.
- I will only eat a thousand calories tomorrow.
- I will write down everything I eat and not go one calorie over.
- If I do go over, I will make up for it by skipping a meal.

The lists were a bit different, but the themes were always the same—controlling, rigid, harsh, and placing all effort and responsibility back on my shoulders to change and perform well enough not to screw up. I hadn't been able to control myself around food since I was a little girl, so I don't know what made me think I could suddenly change. The difference was, I now had to worry about an expanding frame, making the obsession not just about the food, but also about my ever-changing body.

I'd write out my meals and plan out my calories down to the tiniest number. I'd log the food I'd eaten for the day, and if I went over by one calorie, I'd feel so guilty that I'd hit the gym sometimes for six hours at a time, burning thousands of calories—aware of each one as it melted away.

This obsession with food and calories consumed me. My mind was constantly aware of what food was in the room, what food was still on my plate, what food I was going to eat at the next meal, and what food was in the vending machine. Sometimes I couldn't even tell what the person across from me was talking about. My head would race, tormented by the cafeteria buffet that was ten feet away. I thought about what I wasn't going to eat and obsessed about what I was allowed to ingest. I meditated over my next goal and next meal. I gave every last drop of energy and every last moment of my thoughts to one thing and one thing alone.

Food.

I had good foods and bad foods. Good foods were salads, low-fat anything, fruits, veggies, fish, chicken, rice cakes—the usual stuff you would expect beautiful, waif models to eat. Bad foods were everything I loved: pizza, burgers, lasagna, pastas, carbs, chocolates, desserts, Caesar dressing, chips, cheese. If it had any sort of fats or carbs in it or if I really enjoyed it at all, the food went instantly to the terrible list.

In my head, if I messed up with even one bite of something on the bad list, I would fly off the handle and consider the day blown, bingeing on anything and everything, my attitude being "I'll fix it tomorrow and not eat anything." There was no starting over if I had messed up that day. I had no idea how to do that. I was so all-or-nothing that if I got out of my rigid cage for one second, I would go as crazy as I could until the sun went down.

The word "grace" was completely absent from my vocabulary for myself.

THE MONSTER OF ANOREXIA

My body and my emotions were beaten up and exhausted from the spin cycle of obsession. In order to remove this ugly, disgusting monster from my life, I finally decided the best thing to do was to stop eating altogether. I'd been restricting food for a couple of years, but it never seemed to be enough. The mirror was a constant reminder that I was far from my obsessive goal of being painfully thin, and I knew in order to get there I was going to have to do something drastic.

I'd heard of people doing forty-day fasts, so I knew I wouldn't die from one. All kinds of people did it in the Bible—Jesus, Moses—as well as modern-day health gurus, so why couldn't I? The health and spiritual benefits justified my insanity, but ultimately, I wanted to get this ugly beast out of my life. Since I couldn't kill it, I decided to stop feeding it.

I remember walking into my parents' kitchen after finishing my sophomore year, excited to finally be home for the summer. I was on day thirty-seven of absolutely no food other than liquids, and my beautiful mother's face went from an excited smile to a horrified gasp as I walked through our back door.

"Christa, what's happened to you?!" She clasped the sides of her face and examined my emaciated frame.

Because the weight had come off over the course of an entire semester, I hadn't noticed how drastic the change had been. In fact, I was winning the praises of beautiful girls who had noticed my clothes hanging loosely off my fragile body like clothes on a hanger. But Mom hadn't seen me since Christmas, and I was not the same daughter when I walked through her door three months later. I was a skeleton of myself.

My parents sat me down at the dinner table on day thirty-nine, placed a bowl of soup in front of me, and begged me to eat. I loved them and knew they were more than just worried—they were afraid for the life of their only daughter—so I reluctantly put the spoon up to my mouth, feeling like a total failure with each bite.

Something in me expected to be magically cured. I believed deep down that I wasn't going to struggle with food the way I had before—that I had starved the beast and he had died within me. I thought that if I had such self-control that I could eat nothing at all, surely I could have enough self-control to eat small amounts.

Oh, how very wrong I was.

THE MONSTER OF BULIMIA

The day after my starvation fast ended, I found myself in front of a gigantic buffet spread out like the Promised Land before me. When your body hasn't had solid food for a long time, you need to ease yourself back into eating over the course of at least a week or two, beginning with lettuce, maybe a dry potato, increasing bit by bit each day. Of course, I had planned to do this in a list of new rules I had outlined for myself and sworn to keep, but once I held that empty plate in front of a glorious spread of food, giving myself the green light to go, a dry baked potato just wasn't going to cut it. I put a potato on my plate, instantly dousing it with Texas chili. I ate so fast you would have thought I had forgotten how to chew, swallowing entire mouthfuls at a time like a rescued castaway eating her first meal back on the mainland.

Within two minutes of my vacuum-style inhalation, my tiny shrunken stomach began making noises like I was releasing the Kraken. I sprinted to the bathroom as fast as I could, spending the rest of the afternoon on the toilet— crying and beating myself up for ruining all the progress I'd made over the course of the last semester of starvation.

Once again my greatest fear was confirmed. I was, indeed, a failure.

My brain saw only black and white. Either I was the best or I was a loser, and I couldn't take the emotions of the in-between. Remember Ricky Bobby in the Will Ferrell movie *Talladega Nights*? His dad had a bumper sticker that said, "If you're not first—you're last." I laughed when I saw that, then quickly realized, "Oh my gosh. That's actually what I believe about my life."

I had always been first chair in orchestra growing up. My sophomore year in high school I had tried out for all-region orchestra and came in second chair to a girl that everyone knew I was far more advanced than. My body couldn't handle the emotional ramifications of coming in second place. I had a panic attack and passed out, and the paramedics had to be called to take me to the hospital. If I couldn't be the best, I'd just quit, or my body would follow my emotions and physically shut down. The core of my belief system was wired around the fact that my self-worth came solely from my performance, so if my performance resulted in anything but the best, I'd throw in the towel and swing to the opposite extreme, purposely sabotaging everything.

Every part of me fell under this umbrella of lies. I had to perform well for my friends, being the perfect friend, being liked by everyone, and making sure the people around me were happy—most of the time at my expense. If you asked me where I wanted to go for lunch, I'd robotically respond, "Wherever you want to eat." If you asked me what movie I wanted to go see, I'd say, "Whatever movie you want to go see." This was exhausting, of course, and completely unrealistic, resulting in my retreating like a reclusive hermit to my dorm room when my circuits were fried from emotional overloads.

I had to make straight As and was the annoying girl in the front row who knew all the answers, getting in good with every professor. If I could perform well enough in class, I could make the grades I wanted, cutting another notch in my belt of achievement.

I approached my relationship with God in a spirit of performance too, and felt worthy to come to Him, pray to Him, or just be around Him if I'd been good enough. If I hadn't, I would run from Him as fast as I could. This wasn't like the initial encounter I'd had with Him in Canada—with unconditional love and grace. The patterns of my past had come in to choke out the new truth that I had found. Law, rules, and lifeless religion wrapped their iron hands around true freedom in God, cutting off the oxygen from the beautiful grace I'd been given.

After I'd starved myself on and off for a year, my body and stomach were so wrecked that my body stopped working the way it was supposed to. Large chunks of hair fell out of my head, my menstrual cycle was as inconsistent as the weather, and my emotions followed my blood sugar, rising and falling like an elevator on steroids. Once I'd turned on the water faucet and told my body to eat, the floodgate flew open and I found myself powerless to stop or control the amount of food I shoveled in. When you binge on a shrunken stomach that's been in hibernation mode from food for long periods of time, the food can't stay down. My food began coming up on its own. I would binge and have to throw up, not because I shoved two fingers down my throat, but because my body couldn't handle the amount of food I was bulldozing in.

I learned to use this to my advantage.

Instead of trying and failing at starvation, I would binge, feel the drug-like euphoric feeling of control that goes with it, then head to the toilet to throw it all back up.

THE MONSTER OF OVEREATING

I was a college girl striving to make straight As, remain as popular as I could, and fool everyone around me into thinking my life was perfect. But in reality, every day was completely out of control. I'd given up drugs and alcohol. I'd given up cigarettes. I'd given up the things that I knew would lead to addictions that would take years to get free from and were socially frowned upon, but I couldn't give up food. An alcoholic doesn't have to go into a bar to live. He or she can choose to avoid those places. A drug addict can stay away from drug dealers and sketchy street corners. The problem with food was, I had to face my addiction every single day, several times a day, in order to live. On top of that, food is Western culture's acceptable drug.

I think it's interesting how some people will look down their nose at you for having a glass of wine or a beer with your meal, but gorging your brain out at a potluck dinner is completely acceptable. Heading into a casino to escape through gambling is for bottom dwellers and heathens, but drowning your pain in a tub of ice cream is somehow seen as completely normal.

Food is a drug if you use it to self-medicate. Food can hold you in bondage, just like alcohol, smoking, drugs, cutting, sex, pornography, and gambling can. In my journey on this road of addiction, I've come to realize that the danger isn't always in the substance. It's in the abuse of the substance.

Any time I use a substance to escape or to self-medicate my soul, heart, or emotions, to achieve a temporary solution to a bigger problem, I am a slave to that substance, whatever it is. Alcohol abuse isn't worse than food abuse. They both keep you in chains. We have to stop looking at what people are doing and instead ask ourselves why they are doing what they're doing. I had quit getting drunk and smoking cigarettes because that was unacceptable for a so-called good Christian girl, but it didn't mean the root behind why I was getting drunk was completely healed. My addiction had just transferred back to food, and since I didn't have other substances to help me self-medicate, the problem soared off the charts.

You see, it wasn't ever about food. It wasn't ever about any substance. The problem wasn't the external.

The problem was my heart.

My heart was still severely wounded in certain areas, and because I wasn't completely healed, I always needed to find ways to numb the pain and try to fill up the leaky love bucket of my soul.

If you struggle with substance abuse like I did, you will never be free until you go back and open up the vaulted, shameful, dark places of your past and allow yourself to begin the healing process. Then and only then will your behavior change. You will always find something to self-medicate with, whether it be hobbies, addictions, work, substances, obsessions, or lusts. Until you get to the root of why you're self-medicating in the first place, you will find yourself in the same cycle again and again.

Things Have to Change

I had been bingeing and purging for about two years, still restricting when I could, still working out like a mad-woman, and still constantly obsessed with my body, my weight, and food. The summer before my senior year in college, I decided to make a little extra money as a counselor at a sports camp in Missouri. I adored the twelve girls in my cabin, and they hung on my every word, so when one of them walked in as I was throwing up my food in the community bathroom, I completely broke down. I knew these girls were looking up to me as a big sister and role model, watching everything I did with admiration, and something like that had the potential to influence their delicate lives in a devastating way. I couldn't live with that. I wouldn't wish my daily hell on my worst enemy, let alone these girls whom I loved and had been entrusted to take care of.

I looked in the mirror, looked directly into my broken eyes, and made a decision: I had to stop purging, whatever it took. I don't know how I did it, but I did it. I stopped throwing up cold turkey after years of abuse. I couldn't live with myself any other way—pouring myself into these young girls' lives, yet trying to keep this deep, dark secret hidden. The problem with this plan, however, was that I couldn't stop bingeing. My food intake stayed the same, which was out-of-control eating, but I wasn't regulating my weight by throwing up anymore. You can imagine what happened.

The pounds began pouring on.

I hated myself for what I was doing, the way I looked, and the way I felt, but I couldn't risk getting caught purging by the campers. My skin was a mess from the toxins I was putting in my body, and my expanding frame got harder and harder to hide under my once baggy clothes, which were getting tighter every day. Wearing a swimming suit in front of people was enough to make me have a nervous breakdown.

By the time the summer was over and I started my senior year of college, I had gained so much weight that I was embarrassed to even go back to school. My depression was off the charts, but because I was such a people pleaser and perfectionist, no one around me had a clue that anything was wrong, including my roommate. I should have won an Academy Award for my performance—painting on fake smiles and happy faces to fool even those closest to me. This was what was expected of me as a good Christian, or so I thought. I'd get back to my apartment, completely exhausted from being constantly aware of my body and food, finally collapsing in my little twin-size bed. I slowly backed out of social circles and stopped showing up to anything that wasn't required, spending all my spare time in bed or on the couch, watching hours of television late into the night.

The cycle was always the same. I'd turn on the TV to numb my overloaded brain and would see all the beautiful, skinny people and how happy and perfect they seemed. I'd feel so disgusted with myself and my body that I'd end up eating anything and everything I could find, sometimes stealing food from my roommates or neighbors who I knew kept their doors unlocked. I'd make up to ten trips a night down to the vending machine or order a large pizza and eat the whole thing in one sitting. Every time, I felt horrifically shameful and would make more lists of things I was going to do the next day to change myself or to quit doing what I was doing—to try to fix myself. It never worked, though. I always ended up hating myself even more. Sometimes I would lie in bed in the morning, petrified to get up and go into the kitchen, afraid of the damage I was capable of. Was I going to be good? Was I going to go crazy? Could I control myself today?

The days got worse and worse. I slept more and more, and tears finally stopped flowing at all. My heart had hardened and numbed as a last-resort defense mechanism. I would sit on the floor of my kitchen, shoving handfuls of cereal down my throat while crying out to God in the middle of the binge, "Why am I doing this? Why, God? Why can't I stop?" It was like something would come over me to take complete control, and I was held captive inside a body on autopilot. I felt as if I had no choice but to succumb when the pull would lead me, once again, like a slave into the kitchen. What started as a means of feeling in control had turned into a nightmare that was completely out of my control.

This eating disorder was always about power. The amount of food I put into my body was just about the only thing I could control in my life. It was a drug. It felt euphoric. I didn't have power over my sexual abuse or my social status. I didn't have power over my emotions or my appearance, but I could always have power over food. The one thing I had put all my faith in had backfired, and now I was powerless in its cage. I had loved food but it had never loved me back. I had loved controlling food, but in the process, it had started to control me.

I was depressed, powerless, and suicidal. Death would have been easier than the daily hell I was living in, fighting to survive, but longing to just let go. If it all ended, at least I would finally be at peace.

Rock Bottom

I picked up the phone, reluctantly dialing the only number I knew to call, the only place I was ashamed to call. Home.

My body had finally stopped listening to my slave-driving head. I'd drained my precious reserve of performance fuel and found myself void of any desire or ability to get up from an uncomfortable college mattress that had turned into quicksand.

I had finally done it—I had reached the end of me. I cleared my throat, attempting to steady the obvious shake behind each word, but my usual strong voice had disintegrated into a hollow shell of itself.

There would be no faking it today. "Hey, Daddy, it's me."

"Christa?" I felt his immediate fatherly concern. "What's wrong, honey? Are you okay?"

I hesitated for a brief moment, knowing that once the words I feared most came out of my mouth, I could never, ever take them back. They would uncover the one thing I had spent my entire life working overtime to conceal.

I am a failure.

I let out a long, painful sigh. "Dad, I don't think I have the guts to kill myself, but, uh, I need help." My voice trailed off into nothing more than a whisper. "I'm afraid I just don't have the strength to live anymore."

▌ YOUR TURN:
▼ Obsessions

We talked about thoughts in the first chapter, but those thoughts, when left unchecked, can turn into a prison of obsession. For years, I gave the majority of my thought time over to food, working out, my body, and my appearance. But because the bulk of those thoughts were coming from a place of self-hatred and shame, my thoughts never empowered me to move toward healing or permanent change.

Your thoughts will move you and empower you toward something—positive or negative. Whatever you allow to consume your mind, whether it's food, drugs, fear, hate, boys, girls, revenge, anxiety, worry, or love—those thoughts produce actions over and over again. You give power to whatever you focus your mind on.

What thoughts have turned into obsessions?

Is it food? Is it how you're going to lose weight? Is it when you're going to get your next fix? Is it boys? Is it girls? Is it bitterness and hatred? Is it goals? Is it love? Is it acceptance and grace? Is it drugs? Is it fear and worry? Is it sex? Is it money?

You've heard the phrase "You are what you eat." Well, even more than that, "You are what you think." Whatever you allow yourself to meditate on becomes what you worship, and whatever you worship, you become like. Some people think they are at the mercy of their thoughts, but this is completely false. This is why I absolutely love scripture and look at the Bible as a giant book of promises instead of a giant book of rules. When my mind starts to get away from me, I have a few favorite verses about peace and promise that I like to chew on mentally until my emotions change.

Here are just a couple of them.

"The steadfast of mind You will keep in perfect peace, Because he trusts in You" (Isaiah 26:3). I then personalize it: "God, I believe You keep me in perfect peace as my mind is set on You, because I trust in You." I meditate on it until my thoughts and emotions change. I might sing it over and over.

Another favorite verse I turn into personal declaration is Jeremiah 29:11: "I believe You have plans to prosper me and not to harm me—to give me a hope and a future." Saying these words out loud and coming into agreement with the promise (and not with what I feel) bring a peace that passes all understanding.

Are you in bondage to a substance, a thought pattern, an addiction, or depression?

You didn't just wake up one day addicted. You didn't just open your eyes and find yourself at the mercy of depression. You have a lifetime of experiences and beliefs slowly coercing you into a locked cage. A pill might help for a while, but it won't heal—and you deserve to be healed.

But you can't heal your own heart.

If you're struggling with an eating disorder, please find help. Find a therapist, a nutritionist, a friend, a treatment facility, a priest, or a pastor who will help you attack this monster. A lot of you have been trying to battle this on your own, and you can't. You must find someone safe to tell, to confess to, to help you break the shame.

The first step toward healing is venturing out of your

cage and asking someone for help. This might be the hardest thing you've ever done—especially if you're petrified of being anything but perfect. But for you to actually change, you have to face the monster.

And you can't do it alone.

California Sunshine
By *Christa Black*

I can tell you about the rain after forty days of heavy downpour
I can tell you about the clouds, 'cause they just won't go away
And I think it might be just the time to pack my bags and take a
*   ride with you*
Baby, we're both needing something new

CHORUS:
California sunshine's calling my name
Lay me by the ocean, I won't complain
Don't call it a vacation, don't think I ever want to leave
There's nothing like a blue sky over the bay
To let you know that everything is okay
Oh, I just love to get away
To Californ-I-A

I think it's time to slow down, take the top down
Let's go driving all day long
I'm feeling kind of crazy, I think maybe I'm in love
And I wanna turn the music up, tip back my cup
And drink it all in deep
'Cause there's no place on earth I'd rather be

BRIDGE:
Take me surfing, 'cause I've never been
Take me driving down the coast again
Take me high, take me low, just take me out
Let's go dancing down the boulevard
Just bring the night, I just might bring my guitar
It's not too hot, it's not too cold
When it's just right

Chapter 7

Forty Days and a Horse

I walked up the stone path lined with desert flowers to the oversize rustic door, taking a long, deep breath before mustering up the courage to finally walk inside. For the next forty days, this desert treatment facility for eating disorders would be my new home, and I found myself both petrified and relieved to finally arrive. It had been only a few weeks since my dad drove through the night to rescue his suicidal daughter from her senior year of college, so every wound was still fresh and gaping wide. I'd clearly reached the end of my rope, so being at a place that offered a solution to my never-ending nightmare felt like seeing the light at the end of a dark tunnel. At the same time, it meant walking into a foreign land with my dirty laundry and airing it out in front of complete strangers. Not the easiest thing in the world for someone who was prone to hide all signs of weakness and vulnerability.

There were girls there so emaciated and frail that their bones looked as if they'd snap like twigs if you shook their hands. Feeding tubes were shoved up their noses and down into their stomachs for the duration of their stay, allowing machines to automatically feed those unwilling to eat, keeping them alive and filled with nutrients as they slept. Some had cut marks sliced all over their wrists and arms; others had facial hair and masculine mustaches as a result of the anorexia.

One absolutely breathtaking model had abused laxatives for so long, she couldn't go to the bathroom on her own and had to have doctors massage her stomach and remove her fecal matter every few days from her overwrought bowels. Another girl had been abused by a satanic cult for more than a decade, given to them freely by her alcoholic father, who traded her for booze. She gained three hundred pounds in hopes of becoming as unattractive as possible, then swung to the opposite extreme by starving herself on nothing but soup and crackers for an entire year. The weight had come off so quickly that fifty pounds of excess skin hung like draperies on her tiny frame.

Some were obsessive-compulsive, some were paranoid, most were depressed and on medication, but all of us were in the same boat and in need of one thing.

Help.

This was a disease that didn't seem to discriminate. In fact, it took anyone it could as a prisoner. All social classes, age groups, countries, and races were under one roof, one deception, and one addiction. There were wives of preachers and there were Swiss students. There were grandmothers and there were lawyers. Friendships formed between people who would never have given each other a second look in our socially segregated world, but our bonds ran deep and stood true. We all realized very quickly that there was finally no need for the masks we'd grown so accustomed to wearing. These were shameful scars that we had fought to keep as our darkest vaulted secrets, so to be in a place where we were all in the same boat and no one was judging anyone else for being screwed up was absolutely liberating.

We were assigned a therapist, a psychiatrist, a group, a nutritionist, and a horse. The therapist met with you privately several times a week, the psychiatrist evaluated how crazy you were to determine the right meds, the group became your family and support system, the nutritionist outlined a strict eating plan for your specific problem, and the horse became your best friend and worst enemy.

Word on the street was that they paired patients with horses that had similar personalities. I'm not sure how excited I was knowing this, after climbing on top of Willy—the biggest and the most stubborn and disobedient horse in the bunch. When Willy decided he wanted to pee, it didn't matter if he held up the entire line behind him. He'd assume the position and create a small yellow lake for everyone else to walk through. When Willy decided he'd had enough of walking in single file, he'd just stop abruptly or take off through the bush and cactus in the opposite direction. I finally decided I'd had just about enough of this unruly creature and submitted my request for a horse change. They gave me Cedar, a midsize, compliant, mature, and beautiful horse that did anything and everything you told her to do. Now that I look back on it all, I was a perfect mixture of the two extremes: stubborn, strong, and alpha, but so petrified of messing up or disappointing important people that I'd finally comply and obey to go with the flow.

I ventured into new territory with my therapy sessions. These were the first experiences I'd had talking with anyone about my problems, instead of trying to hide them. Up until this point, I had no idea why $A + B = C$. I just knew I was living with C (my addiction), and that C was a daily living hell. I'd never really given much thought as to what As and Bs had actually produced C.

My therapist was sent from God. He prodded and poked around in my past, asking pointed, yet careful questions about my childhood and my parents, scribbling illegibly on a large yellow pad as I blabbered away. He had a safe and gentle way about him, making it easy for me to spill every secret I'd ever had. I realized quickly that he liked to park on the same ending question. "And how did that make you feel, Christa?"

This question astounded me. I had never really thought about how my past made me feel. I never reasoned why certain personality traits had been produced. I never wondered if there was something behind the behavior, fears, addictions, and depression. The more we talked, the more I understood. The more I opened up, the more the reasons why became illuminated. It was like a huge map was being drawn, and I was finally seeing how pieces of my past needed to be healed in order to change behaviors in the future.

My addiction to food wasn't a complete mystery anymore, and my heart finally made sense, with the help of forty hours of therapy a week—and a horse.

Stripped Bare

I nearly had a heart attack the first time I was required to walk into the nurse's station and weigh in with the resident nurse. Once a week, we had to have our weight logged, and I quickly learned that in order to refrain from bursting into tears and wanting to die, it was a good idea for me to just turn around and not look at the number on the scale. I was definitely one of the biggest girls among the anorexic waifs and ultrathin bulimics, having stopped purging the summer before. I felt like the walking physical example of the extra layers most girls were petrified of becoming. This definitely didn't make my predicament any easier, producing deep wells of determination to get this problem fixed.

On top of that, the rule of the house was that every girl had to clear her plate completely at each meal. This had never been a problem for me. I'd inhale my food in record time and have to sit and watch the anorexic beside me cut her food into hundreds of pieces while slowly eating each bite, longing to take over for her (and the girl next to her, and the girl next to her). By week two of this eating routine, I realized that the structure they had in place was doing nothing to help the bulimics and overeaters. It was aiding only the anorexics. I fought the system, finally receiving special approval to be able to leave one bite of each item on my plate.

This was actually a greater feat for me than scaling Mount Everest. I was so consumed and obsessed with food that leaving even one bite of anything on my plate was out of the question. In fact, I couldn't even remember a time when I needed a takeaway box at a restaurant or left half a candy bar in the wrapper. I inhaled food like a vacuum. In my book, food wasn't meant for enjoyment—it was made to be destroyed, and I had years of practice annihilating any food I found in front of me. My first few attempts at trying to leave food on my plate left me ready to explode. I'd finally end up dousing the last few bites in salt or smashing them into a disgusting pile to try to make them less appealing.

Two hours after each meal, the toilet monitor had to go into the bathroom after you "did your business" and flush for you. They weren't taking any chances on the bulimics, although every once in a while you'd find a nasty little present behind a couch or out in the bushes. Shaving razors and sharp objects were confiscated to make sure that no one had any "accidents," which made for some hairy women walking around, but we didn't seem to care. All decisions were removed, except for the decision to fully participate and engage in our therapy, making the burdened fear of daily food turmoil a distant memory.

I'd never felt so safe in my life. Every part of my day and night was completely controlled. I had nurses telling me when to wake up and checking on me several times during the night to make sure I was in bed. I had a specific schedule and was required to attend and participate in my agenda for the day. And most important, there was no way to get my drug. There was no way to sneak it in. We were out in the middle of the desert surrounded by miles of cactus. There were no loopholes or ways for bulimics or overeaters to binge—the kitchen was locked tight. For the anorexics wanting to restrict food by refusing to eat, the staff would just hook them up to feeding tubes to give them their necessary nutrients. Finding a way around your particular problem was pretty much impossible.

Food had been my constant control since I was a little girl, and now the one thing I had been accustomed to running to, I couldn't run to anymore. I was learning the reasons why I ran to food in the first place and discovering and unearthing deep emotional wounds from my past. But emotions weren't always stable, as rumbling took place in the depths of my soul. Now that food was outside of my reach (as were drugs, and alcohol, and music), the only thing I had left in my bag of tricks was the one thing I had started with.

Performance.

TRANSFERENCE

At this point in my life, my addictions knew how to jump. They jumped from performance when I was a child, to food when I was a kid, to alcohol when I was an adolescent, to cigarettes when I was a teenager, to drugs when I was a high school student, to destructive music when I was depressed, back to food when I was in college, eventually dead-ending in performance. It was all I could get my hands on. The addictions and the coping mechanisms jumped (and would have continued to jump) until the reasons behind them were finally healed. This is why I'm hammering this subject home. You need to see that until the roots are pulled out, you will continue to find ways to self-medicate until you are healed.

I have a good friend who was a terrible drug and alcohol addict while growing up. Some of her stories would make your eyes bulge in disbelief at her sheer stupidity and unnecessary near-death encounters. And while she has been through drug and alcohol rehab and would consider herself clean (hitting up AA meetings and following the program to the letter), she finds herself enslaved to food on a daily basis, unsatisfied with and angry at her weight and her inability to find freedom in this area. People praise her all the time for saying no to a drink or walking the other way when substance abuse is involved, but there's a distinct correlation between shutting down a couple of addictions and keeping another one wide-open.

The heart behind the addiction hasn't been healed. This is what I found very clearly in rehab. Every addiction had been closed off to me, except for performance, so what did I do?

I performed.

There were different levels of achievement and privilege, depending on how long you had been there and how much you had improved while cooperating with the program. Everyone started as a Level 1, and we progressed in stages as we accomplished certain tasks at the discretion of our therapists. Our privileges increased with each level, and since my entire life had been about achieving and becoming the best, I approached my treatment in the exact same way.

My forty days became a race to beat everyone and run the course in an impressively fast amount of time, breaking any and all records and proving to those around me that I was strong and capable. I knew exactly what I needed in order to move forward. Once I figured out the formula and the program (how to go back to my past and find painful and traumatic circumstances and then forgive and replace in order to heal), I set out to remove the thorns and move on faster than anyone else.

I ran into rehab with exactly the same attitude with which I ran through life. I was going to go for it, beat it, and conquer it. I was going to impress and astound all the doctors, walking out of those doors after my forty-day adventure never to struggle again. I was going to be the poster child for perfect freedom—black and white—all or nothing. There was no such thing as grace for the journey. I was either perfect or a failure. The day was either a success or a disaster. Either I was healed or I was still broken.

The problem with this approach to healing is that I never allowed myself to get really honest with what was inside. I didn't have time to. Being perfect around my addiction was the goal, and getting to that goal was ground I had to attain, so I passed up crucial steps of healing along the way. I never allowed myself to just be. If I had a bad day, I had to get out of it as quickly as possible and move on to the next mountain. If I uncovered something dirty from my past, I had to just say the words to forgive and heal fast, moving on at lightning speed.

THE MUSIC BEGAN

My best friend and ally in treatment was an unlikely candidate, but we stuck together like two mismatched pieces of Velcro. She was tall and beautifully statuesque with golden, natural blond hair and long eyelashes that flapped like butterfly wings when she blinked. Her laugh was contagious and her personality bigger than life itself. Without ever trying to be anything extraordinary, she couldn't help it. She just was. I was instantly drawn to her, and she to me, even though our backgrounds were about as different as two foreign languages.

I was raised a preacher's daughter in a small West Texas town, and her family owned an entire cove on the ocean in the Hamptons along with two breathtakingly large Manhattan apartments with live-in servants. My family went camping at the lake for a summer vacation, and her family visited their relatives in European castles. I was a hodgepodge of heritage. She was German royalty. My parents cashed in their savings to get me admitted, and she told her family she was going on a holiday around the world and wrote a small check for the thirteen-hundred-dollar-a-day treatment facility.

Alexandra was most definitely unlike any friend I'd ever had before.

We had a certain amount of free time every day. Some spent the afternoon reading; others chatted and compared stories. The women who had been there the longest, and who therefore claimed dibs on the television remote, were addicted to the Game Show Network and were obsessed with reruns of *Family Feud*. One of the newer and nicer nurses brought her guitar from time to time, and since my dad had taught me five chords the previous summer, I decided I'd take a stab at songwriting to pass the free time.

I'd steal away and write songs that identified with our present situation—snapshots that gave expression and release to my pain. The first song I wrote was appropriately named "Forty Days" and was my first attempt to find a creative outlet to help me deal with my journey. It felt liberating to create something beautiful from the ugly battlefield of my past. I would work for hours at a time, then yank Alexandra into a side room while nervously hammering through my new masterpiece. Her first reaction was not exactly what I had expected.

"Christa!" She stood as she spoke, her voice escalating into an excited scream. "The world has to hear this story! The world has to hear this music!"

I'd just laugh at her and shrug my shoulders. I'd never thought about being a professional musician. It was just too risky a profession, and I needed certain assurances in my life. There was no way I would ever voluntarily take the level of risk or submit to the possibility of failure that a musician has to constantly go through. But something in me loved that she believed in me, and deep down, I started wondering if the one thing I had always loved the most— music—could be something I could jump off the cliff for, something I could try for a living.

In the deep corridors of a heart conditioned not to dream too loudly, I secretly hoped it could be.

FAMILY

I know I've been richly blessed in the family department. I couldn't have asked for a more loving, consistent, support- ive family to be born into. But even the most incredible families have problems. You can't live conflict-free in close proximity with the same group of people for that many years on end. It's impossible. You show me a family that doesn't have any conflict, and I'll go find you a unicorn.

There were many external factors helping to mold the broken girl I had become, so it was inevitable that some of those issues originated in the home. I had lived the majority of my life there. Some problems were just misunderstand- ings, and some were stupid mistakes made while we were all growing into maturity. Others were wounds that hadn't been fully worked out and allowed to heal, but I'm blessed to say that not one problem in my family was malicious.

I know this wasn't the case for many of my fellow patients. Every single girl in that treatment facility had fam- ily issues—from being raped by relatives to being neglected in favor of money and status. And every single issue, big or small, needed to be addressed and worked through. With the navigation of our therapist captains, we traipsed back through the muddy waters of distant memories.

My mom and I are a lot alike. I get my passion from her, which I love. When you have two passionate people living under one roof, though, there are bound to be some fireworks. She's very headstrong, driven, and powerful, which is where I learned my determination. When my mom sets her mind to do something, just try to stand in her way. Mountains don't intimidate her heart, impossibility doesn't faze her will, and just because someone's never done something before doesn't mean she won't charge forward to conquer the challenge with fearless courage.

She was forced to watch the women in the generation before her get stepped on, devalued, thrown into the housewife role (whether they liked it or not), and required to be seen and treated by society as the weaker, lesser sex. The passionate heart that God created her with couldn't accept this constricted, unjust fate, so with fearless passion she swore to never be trampled on or controlled like many of the women she saw around her.

That inner vow created strength and determination, but it also created a woman ready to fight.

And then here I came. I had a hot, redheaded temper, I was already jealous of her head-turning natural beauty, and we were equally matched in personality, passion, and drive. Neither of us knew how to back down from a squabble, even after discovering that we were wrong. We'd go for the kill and fight for the win, regardless of whether we deserved the title. A lot of times, we'd rather be right than have a relationship.

My anger was aimed toward her for as long as I could remember. I judged her strength, completely oblivious to all the societal issues the women in her generation had to overcome just to be heard and recognized. I was furious at her thick skin—unaware of how that armor had been her best defense against years of harsh words, especially living as a pastor's wife. I was livid at her pride, blinded to the drive that forged her groundbreaking determination.

The more I allowed anger, bitterness, and an unforgiving heart to fester inside, the more my worst nightmare became true. When you allow judgment to consume you, one of two things tends to happen: Either you become the polar opposite of what you hate, or you become what you hate. I hated that my mother was extremely opinionated, strong, and determined. I was mad at her for being, at times, controlling, unbending, and unmoved. But I didn't ever stop and ask her what had made her that way. I just judged the woman I saw in front of me. My judgment sentence, however, eventually backfired. The more I focused my negative magnifying glass on what I saw as her shortcomings, the more I became the exact things I was focusing on.

I was unbending. I was prideful, especially when she was around. I was determined to be ridiculously strong and capable. I was stubborn. My worst fear was being seen as weak. I hated admitting I was wrong. And I was definitely controlling.

The guy who sexually abused me wasn't around anymore, nor were the mean boys who liked to poke fun and call names. The neglectful friends and the harsh critics weren't available. The one person who was ready to walk beside me through the fire, ready to do whatever it took to see her only daughter free, ready to cash in her inheritance money just to send me to rehab—was the person sitting right in front of me. And because she was a tangibly available target to aim at, I did just that.

I angrily pointed my gun, set my sights, and, drawing a huge bull's-eye on my poor mom, fired away.

My parents traveled from Texas to participate in the family-week portion of my rehab, and I was ready and waiting to hurl my huge bag of stones. My mother sat across

from me during our family therapy session—dumbfounded
and completely broken over any turmoil that she could have
possibly caused her only daughter, whom she loved so desperately. She'd never meant to hurt me. She had developed
certain characteristics for her own survival, just as I had. It
was never her intention to wound or cause heartbre

With my therapist as the mediator, we has h away
at it for hours, revisiting painful memories and   ch ng-
ing family dynamics. A box of tissues had bee n em d,
bandages were ripped off, and at the close of ur se n,
with oceans of sincerity in her teary eyes, Mom confeed
her deepest regrets as a parent and pleaded for my forgiveness. Through violent sobs and a melted heart , I repeted
"yes" over and over as we embraced. I begge d the ame
question of her—for years of defiant, rebelli ous, hteful
behavior—and she hastily agreed.

All seemed to be right and good with the world for a
moment. A huge thorn had been yanked from the depth
of my core and filled with the most unexplainable peace.
This forgiveness felt better than any drug I'd ever tried,
better than any anger I had held on to, better than any
revenge my soul had fed on.

It felt like I had finally found the eye of the storm.

FORGIVENESS

Forgiveness. What a superhuman concept.

If it was left up to my will, I know I would never have
the strength or ability to fully forgive. When something
painful happens, human nature tends to want to hold on
to the resulting bitterness and anger as long as possible.
It's infinitely harder to overlook an offense than to get
angry and bitter. Bitterness is easy—forgiveness is anything but.

For years my merciless heart was on lockdown. I didn't

want to budge, or at least my pride didn't want to budge. I couldn't see how letting go and letting someone off the hook would do any good at all. I burned with a fire for justice. I wanted the person who had hurt me to hurt the way I had, which somehow justified my anger. I threw verbal punches and held on to bitterness. I kept blaming—kept pointing the finger. I wanted someone to pay.

When we refuse to let go of anger, in any circumstance, the only one really shackled to the poison of anger and bitterness is the one consumed by it. In fact, refusing to forgive someone is like drinking poison and then waiting for your spited adversary to die.

The boy who sexually abused me wasn't handcuffed to my wrath. I was. The kids who hurt and rejected me weren't overwhelmed with unforgiveness. I was. My family wasn't living under the power of my hatred. I was.

When someone says the words "I will never forgive you for what you did to me," the only person who has to carry the burden of that heavy load is the one administering the sentence.

But mercy triumphs over judgment.

Kindness brings people into true sorrow for what they have done.

A lot of people think they have to feel like forgiving before they even start the process, but most times, it's not going to happen that way. Waiting until you feel like forgiving someone who has wronged you will be like waiting for a cake to bake outside of the oven. It's not going to happen. The guilty can sometimes be far from deserving the precious gift being bestowed upon them.

But forgiving those who have wronged you sets you free.

I recently heard a story about a woman whose daughter had been brutally raped and murdered by a group of young men. When the men were eventually caught and charged with the crime, the mother's reaction astounded a nation. She forgave them all. Now, the very men who raped and murdered her daughter were so transformed by her act of kindness and forgiveness, they now work for her. She even considers them to be her sons.

There is more transforming and life-giving power in forgiveness than in anger. There is more might and strength in mercy than in bitterness. There is more release and freedom in pardon than in judgment.

When forgiving those who had wronged me felt more impossible than picking up a mountain with my bare hands, it meant I hadn't known forgiveness enough to then return the favor. Forgiveness is one trait that doesn't seem to come very naturally to human nature. It's something that has to be learned and sometimes willed over deep antagonistic emotions.

Most of us have a hard time forgiving those around us because of one thing: We really haven't forgiven ourselves. If you ask people if they have any regrets, heads tend to bow in shame as painful memories punch the gut. My list was long and ugly, and I hated myself for it. I locked my terrible shortcomings away, fighting desperately to keep them a secret or living to overcome their shame. I hated myself for having done things that were absurdly stupid, or for looking the way I did, or acting in ways I hated.

When you refuse to forgive yourself for being the way you are, doing the things you do, or never doing or being enough, you make it almost impossible to change. Loving and forgiving yourself where you are, at this very moment, is the starting point for moving forward and changing everything.

FREEDOM

I complied with the treatment program completely. I did everything my therapist, psychiatrist, and leaders told me to do. I played the perfect patient role to a T—until one statement got thrown like a monkey wrench at my gut. There was just one sentence that I kept hearing over and over that I simply refused to accept. "You will always deal with this addiction at some level and in some capacity for the rest of your life."

I just couldn't come to terms with this statement. I wasn't okay that from birth I had been struggling and in pain. I wasn't all right with the fact that because of things outside of my control, I was just going to have to accept that it was my lot in life to suffer in some capacity forever. I refused to believe I would have to be on the defensive as I walked into every kitchen, restaurant, or Christmas dinner. I had believed so many lies in my lifetime that this one wasn't going to find its way in. I was determined about that.

The performer in me battled this statement for the wrong reasons, but the spirit in me fought for the right ones. I'd seen a powerless God in a lot of the church, where scripture was justified to fit lack and pain instead of the radical, uncomfortable, mind-bending antics that Jesus displayed. Scripture said that Jesus healed every single person he came to out of compassion. Talk about radical. He taught unexplainable peace and eternal joy. He spoke about conquering death and living in total freedom. I didn't need a bunch of rules to follow. I didn't need a box to fit into.

I needed something bigger than I was.

I needed power.

I needed deliverance.

Today I am proud to say, I am absolutely, miraculously, 100 percent free from my food addiction. And I don't just mean sometimes free. I mean all-the-time free. You can ask my husband, my friends, my family, and the people I tour with. They'll all tell you the same thing: Christa does not have food issues.

In fact, I have to try hard to remember what it felt like to be enslaved to food on a daily basis. I still have the memory of it, but the feelings don't compute. Freedom tastes so good that it has completely obliterated any and all recollection of the terrifying trauma I used to live in every single day, facing every single meal.

I tell you this not to boast. I don't write these words to shove my freedom in your face. I'm encouraging you—this is your future too. It's not just for me; it's for every single one of you that has battled this horrifying life killer, or any terrible addiction that steals your peace and keeps you in chains.

I didn't have a lot of road maps on my journey to liberation or people pointing out the way to go. In-patient treatment opened the door to why I had this addiction and started the ball rolling, but it definitely didn't fix me permanently. Something—or Someone—way more powerful had to do that, and continues to do that every day.

If you're battling any kind of substance abuse or addiction, you don't have to live in hell anymore. You don't even have to manage your problem anymore. Managing pain is not freedom, and it just isn't good enough. Freedom, however, doesn't come without a fight. A lifetime of memories, experiences, thought patterns, words, and actions have made you the person you are now. Getting out of those mental chains means going to war, and my prayer is that the layers of this book are helping you learn how to not only fight this battle, but also win.

I finally put my foot down. Addictions would no longer transfer in my life. I was going after the heart of the problem, which was the leaky bucket of my wounded heart. I started battling my thinking, which changed my beliefs, which altered my feelings, which began producing entirely different actions. In the process, I was pulling out old painful roots, being loved, and learning how to be forgiven, how to forgive myself, and then how to forgive others.

Believe me, if I can do it, you can do it too.

The first step in the twelve-step program is admitting that you are powerless over your addiction and that your life has become unmanageable. This step is usually not very hard to admit when everything is spiraling downward. The second one is my favorite: "Come to believe that a Power greater than ourselves can restore us to sanity."

I like to add on to that one a little bit: "and completely deliver us from our chains and totally set us free." I know the reason I'm free from this addiction is not because I did all the right things, or because I had the best therapist, or because I'm stronger than others. I believe I'm free because I believed God. I believed Him when He said He came to set me free (John 8:36). I believed Him when He said that He came to give me a hope and a future—and there wasn't much hope or future in addiction and depression (Jeremiah 29:11). I believed Him when He said that He would never leave me or forsake me; that He comforts me when I cry; that the old has passed away, and I am now a new creation (Deuteronomy 31:8; Matthew 5:4; 2 Corinthians 5:17). I believed Him when He said he loved me, and that nothing I ever did could separate me from that love (Romans 8:38–39).

Believing Him was the first part, experiencing Him was the second, and receiving grace for the journey (the mess-ups, the highs and the lows, the consistent failures) was the third. I always thought grace was this weak little word. I thought it meant that I was just pardoned and forgiven, but it's infinitely bigger than that. The grace of God is His literal power to change and transform. I couldn't change myself. I wasn't strong enough. The more I threw myself into the arms of His powerful grace when I wanted to go binge or restrict or purge, knowing that I wasn't strong enough to say no or to resist the familiar temptations, the more I realized it was actually the smartest thing I've ever done. It was admitting my weakness that allowed

Him to finally come in and be strong. It was in my surrender that He was able to fight on my behalf.

I can't begin to tell you how many times the overwhelming feeling of helplessness would come over me, and I'd scream out loud, "God, I literally don't have the strength to choose to do the right thing here. You're going to have to come in and do this for me!"

A lot of you don't need another list of things to do—you need real power. Well, I just happen to know the most powerful guy in the universe, who actually wants you free more than you want it yourself.

Surrender that power to Him right now. Hand over your failures, your addictions, your depression, and your chains. Lay them in His hands and confess your need for a power greater than yourself to come in and set you free. Say it out loud. Scream it at the top of your lungs. Let Him take you back to painful memories and then release your pain in the arms of a Father that has only ever loved you, wanted a relationship with you, and wanted to teach you how amazing you are so you can live life completely free and empowered.

If you find yourself struggling seconds later, surrender again. If it all comes back in five minutes, surrender again. Every time you feel the need or urge to run to old patterns of destructive behavior, throw your hands in the air and give up, again and again, as many times as it takes. God never tires as you offer your precious sacrifice of surrender. In fact, He lives to rescue you.

Freedom is yours, friends. Complete freedom. Don't you dare settle for anything less.

↓ YOUR TURN:
Granting an Undeserved Pardon

Forgiving someone without being forgiven is difficult. It's almost impossible to give away something you haven't received.

Do you need to be forgiven? Ask God now.

God's forgiveness is so powerful, and He has oceans of grace and mercy ready to pour out over you. It really doesn't matter what you've done, even though you might think it does. There's not one thing that you could do, no matter how terribly horrendous, that can separate you from the love of the God who made you.

When I realized my need for a higher power, and for a God who not only loved me and was for me, but also forgives me so thoroughly that I have absolutely no reason to be mad at myself ever again, my whole life changed. I could finally relax. When you are unconditionally forgiven, you forgive unconditionally. When I let God forgive me, then forgave myself, it became natural to forgive those around me.

It brings life, then extends life to others. It sets me free and sets others free.

Do you need to forgive yourself?

Are there things about yourself that you hate? What parts of your past have you not been able to move past?

Did you cheat on your husband or wife, boyfriend or girlfriend? Did you betray a family member? Are you ashamed that you haven't become more or have given up on your dreams? Whatever it is, it's holding you up and keeping you in a yoke of slavery. Forgiving yourself, even if it was your fault, is one of the most important things you can ever do. If you're blaming, judging, or living in self-hatred and shame, you will never be free. Ever. You will never become the person you want to become. You will never experience the peace that passes all understanding.

Go find a mirror, look deep into the eyes of the one that you might have despised, and let yourself go free. Speak to yourself. Speak a pardon; let yourself off the hook; let yourself finally be free from your own judgment and condemnation.

Forgive yourself.

This is painful and might take a lot of time and repetition. Choosing to forgive yourself for the things you've done wrong and are ashamed of isn't easy, but you have to start somewhere.

And that somewhere is here and now.

Write down the name of anyone you either haven't forgiven or don't believe you can ever forgive.

When we refuse to forgive those who have hurt us, we are the ones who stay crippled—tethered to an act that is long over. Some hearts get hard, shutting off and building up high walls. Others retreat in fear of the same thing happening again, but when bitterness begins to creep in, it pollutes the soul.

My first list was long and difficult. I had a lot of people who had hurt me, and I was holding on with a death grip to that hurt. It's time to begin the process of letting these people go. It's time to detox from the poison. You deserve to be free of that burden. You deserve to live your life without the cage of bitterness.

They might not deserve your pardon, but *you* deserve your pardon.

You may not feel anything but numbness and anger in the beginning, but I've learned to fake it till I make it. Forgiveness isn't usually a onetime thing, especially with deep wounds. When the emotions of hate and bitterness come up again, you have to willfully push them aside and choose to forgive again—sometimes on a moment-by-moment basis.

Ask God for help. He's ready to help you. Ask Him to show you what forgiveness looks like so you can learn to forgive. Forgiveness isn't natural—it's supernatural. Be honest. Tell Him how hard it is to forgive the one who raped you, the one who ruined your life, the one who might still torment you. Just talk to Him. Ask Him for help. He's the King of forgiveness, and He's waiting for you to ask for His wisdom and power in this situation.

Go down the list and verbally speak out your forgiveness toward those who have wronged you. Cry if you need to. Scream. But choose to start this process—even if you feel the exact opposite.

Repeat these words.

"I choose to forgive you, _____, for _____, and I release you, and I release myself from the chains of my bitterness and unforgiveness."

You might not feel a thing, but just try. Try to start this crucial process in moving toward freedom.

I promise you, freedom is worth it.

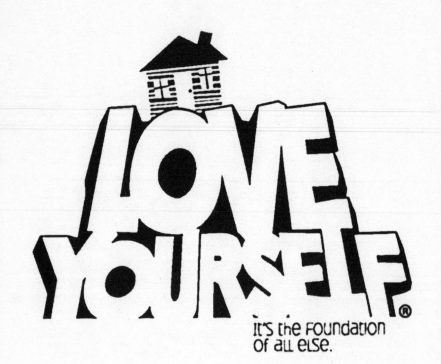

LOVE YOURSELF®

iT'S THE FOUNDATION
OF ALL ELSE.

Lonely
By Christa Black and Ryan Smith

A thousand faces—I have known a thousand smiles
I have tasted happiness I can't describe
But I've lived a lifetime of moments without you
I can't help but wonder when this road will end
When you'll find me—when our journey will begin
Living out a lifetime of moments beside you
When will this aching in my heart begin to fade
I'm trying to be strong—I'm trying not to break

CHORUS:
'Cause I'm lonely—I'm lonely for you
I'm lonely

Destiny, come, hold me while I am alone
Even though I know you're always in control
I could use your sweet words that always remind me
I still believe this path I'm walking on is right
And yet my heart is torn 'cause you're not by my side

CHORUS:
'Cause I'm lonely—I'm lonely for you
I'm lonely
I'm lonely for your heartbeat to beat along with mine
I'm lonely for you

Chapter 8

Lessons in Love

After rehab, I decided to try some cliff jumping into the unknown. Not literally, of course, but that might have actually been easier than rewiring my brain for the uncertain. To my relief and surprise, not only did I survive the leap, but I also discovered an unexplored knack for risk taking.

Living as a musician was never consistent work, and it was just about as unpredictable as the weather, but I had found the reason I was put on this earth. Making music, writing, singing, and performing in front of thousands of people was the easiest thing I'd ever done, and with it came a joy that was deep and peacefully settling. The fact that someone would pay me for it was just icing on the cake.

After moving from Nashville to New York, then back to Nashville, then to London for a year on my musical escapades, I once again moved back to the familiar soil of Nashville, spending my days writing and surfing the Internet at my favorite Music City coffee shop—Fido. One sunny afternoon as I walked into my usual hangout with a friend, I somehow locked eyes with a hunky guy with rippling biceps and sporting long hair. He shook my hand and introduced himself, both of us acting as awkward as sixth graders discovering that the opposite sex didn't, in fact, have cooties. I couldn't think of anything clever or brilliant to say, so with the grace and charm of a toad, I lifted up the side of my shirt to show him my latest skate-boarding hip bruise. How charming. He excused himself and hurriedly packed up his belongings to rush outside and jump on his huge orange motorcycle and race away.

My friend asked me, "Who in the world was that?" "I don't really know," I replied curiously as he sped off. "Just a guy who Myspace messaged me the other day." Lucas had moved to town while I lived in London and started to hang out with some friends of mine. One girl in particular had suggested that we might get along, so he read a few of my blogs on Myspace and commented on them, introducing himself briefly, but that was the end of it. Neither of us had thought much of it, and we hadn't made any plans to ever actually meet. It had just…happened.

The moment we made each other's random acquaintance that unexpected day in the coffee shop, he left immediately to make a couple of phone calls—one to his mother, the other to his best friend. He informed them of the dire situation, letting them know they needed to get ready. As he touched my hand that day, he knew.

He had just met the girl he was going to spend the rest of his life with.

REARVIEW MIRROR

As a single woman, I never had any problems in the heart-palpitating, butterflies-in-your-stomach, attracted-to-any-thing-cute-that-moved department.

Every restaurant, airport, grocery store, and church gathering I went to, my hot-guy radar was on ten, constantly scoping out anyone who might fit the bill. I was always aware of what guys were looking at me and what guys weren't looking at me, and my emotions teetered in the balance between the two extremes.

If they weren't looking, I was depressed and felt ugly.

If they were looking, I was nervous and had no idea how to act. I never seemed to be able to win.

My deepest desire was to have a relationship with a man. The problem with this desire was that men had been the greatest source of my pain, from abuse to rejection to everything in between. It's very interesting when the one thing you want more than anything in the world is the one thing that's hurt you more than anything in the world. If that's not proof that we're wired for love, I don't know what is—constantly wanting to play with fire, knowing you could get burned. After being rejected for years, I had finally convinced myself that I didn't need men at all. This conclusion wasn't what I really wanted. It was a crazy attempt to protect my already wounded heart from even more disaster.

I was driving my car one night, frustrated and broken-hearted that I was headed to yet another wedding while flying solo, and all of a sudden it hit me like a ton of bricks.

I was attracting exactly what I believed I deserved: nothing.

I went on one date in high school. He was a drug dealer who cut our date short to go make some money when his beeper went off. I went to prom alone, assuring everyone that I wanted it that way because my nonexistent college boyfriend wasn't able to make it. And I had fallen hard for a musician who loved keeping me up all night to talk, only to find out I was his emotional and intellectual crutch while he dated a blonde whom he'd rather not talk to. The two of them had make-out activities on the agenda.

Because I believed I wasn't worthy of romantic love, guys weren't seeing me in the romantic category. Because I believed I wasn't very attractive, guys didn't seem to be very attracted to me. Because I believed in and prided myself on my fierce independence (how I could always carry my own suitcase, change my own tire, and do anything and everything any guy could do), they treated me accordingly. I believed I didn't really need a man, so when a man isn't needed, one doesn't need to come around.

I did believe I was a good friend, so I had heaps of guy friends. I also believed I was just one of the guys, so I was always invited to hang out. But every time a cute guy would get close, my head and heart would scream, "Please don't reject me! I know you probably will! Please don't reject me! I know you probably will!"

It's almost like they could somehow hear my thoughts as radio beacons projected into the cosmos, warning them of the land mines up ahead.

And because my head and heart were a complete rejected mess, my actions would immediately follow their lead. I believed that I would eventually get rejected, so any time I got wind of a possible rejection, I would beat the guy to the punch and reject him first. In fact, you could always tell when I was into a guy. I would turn into a complete ogre—picking on everything he did, making fun of his every move, and cutting him down at every possible opportunity. My crushes definitely felt crushed, over and over again. If for some reason he did stick around after all my knives had been thrown, I would usually just run away as fast as I could or disappear completely.

My experience with rejection as a kid was defining my love life as an adult, even though I was a completely different person inside and out. I was still letting insecure, pubescent, pimple-faced bullies determine everything about my romantic future. I was letting terrible things that happened long ago continue to dictate what was happening in the present, and because I approached every guy through a lens of rejection, rejection was exactly what I got.

It was time to make a change.

In my car that evening on the way to that wedding, I tilted my tiny rearview mirror down so I could look into my sad, lonely, exhausted green eyes, and I began to speak.

"Christa Black, I believe you are worthy of love. I

believe your heart is worthy of holding. I believe you don't have to be so independent anymore out of fear. You want someone to take care of you, and I believe you're worth taking care of. I believe you can do most things on your own, but you don't have to do them on your own anymore. I believe you're an attractive woman. I believe you're not just the best friend. I believe you will be married someday to someone you want to be married to. I believe someone will love you—because, Christa, you love yourself."

The air shifted. I literally felt a peace fall in the atmosphere as I drove along. The cloud that always rained on my parade and blurred my vision instantly lifted, and every hair on my arms stood on end as if I was in the middle of a moment so important, breathing might be seen as an interruption. I felt life pouring into my soul—life that I had longed for—as an ancient paradigm moved toward a greater truth than the one I had been a slave to.

As long as I live, I will never, ever forget what happened the very next day. I walked into the same coffee shop I always walked into, wearing the same old dress I had worn a million times, with the same haircut, the same face, and exactly the same weight. But this time as I walked through the front door, every single guy in that place looked up and stared at me. (And I am not exaggerating.) For a minute, I thought maybe I had tucked my dress into my underwear again. It wouldn't have been the first time. But they weren't looking at me because I was embarrassing, ugly, or wrong. In fact, I could feel their admiration and not necessarily their lust. My newly confident demeanor noticeably turned head after head as I walked to the counter to stand in line and order my usual coffee.

I had started to believe I was beautiful, so I felt beautiful and in turn began acting beautiful. When you act beautiful, people see you as someone beautiful. When you act like you're someone of great worth, people treat you like you're someone of great worth.

Spirit, aura, persona—call it what you like—but I was projecting something unseen into that room, something stronger than my natural body, and I watched as every man heard the new message loud and clear and responded accordingly.

Absolutely nothing in the physical realm had changed. I looked the same, I sounded the same, and my circumstances were still the same, but I definitely wasn't the same. My heart and my perception had illuminated and been transformed. I had started believing I was different. I had started believing the truth. And because I finally believed I was someone worthy of love, in the humblest words possible, guys couldn't seem to keep their eyes off me.

You will attract what you believe you deserve. If you believe the guy you want will never want you back, then he won't. If you believe you're worth being beaten up on, then you will continue to attract the same lowlife who will hit you. If you believe you're always going to be the friend and not the lover, then you will continue to be the friend. If you believe you can't get a guy to love you unless you have sex with him, then you'll get sex and not always love.

The person you see in front of you, who could be coming after you romantically, might be the exact definition of what you believe you deserve. The person might be amazing, loving, and kind, or perhaps cruel, demeaning, and harsh. The person could be faithful, or perhaps a cheat. The person might be supportive and protective or abusive and damaging.

If you don't like the person you see sitting across from you, you might need to look in the mirror and do what I did. You might need to start speaking the opposite over your life—to find out the truth and release it into your heart and soul.

You might need a perception makeover.

THE X-FACTOR

I've met breathtakingly gorgeous models who were the ugliest girls in the world, and outwardly ordinary girls who were the most gorgeous beings on the planet. They say that beauty is only skin-deep, and my experience has been that true beauty is definitely more in the mind and heart than it is the eyes. When the heart believes beauty, beauty is created.

Have you ever met a girl that guys get silly around? From the outside, the girl doesn't stick out like a super-model, but you wouldn't know it from the way guys fumble over their words when they get near her. She's not the prettiest girl or the thinnest or the best dressed. She just has this thing about her that makes guys go weak at the knees.

She has the X-factor.

I've had several friends like this in my life. There was one girl in college that made every guy blush like a little schoolboy. Physically speaking, she didn't have the best body, amazing clothes, or a perfect face. She just carried this radiance about her that was incredible. It was so stable and secure, but also approachable and honoring. Boys felt like men around KT because she made them feel that way. It wasn't manipulating or self-serving—she just knew who she was enough to make people comfortable around her. Guys fought to escort her to school dances and battled for dates because they longed to guard and value a girl who valued herself.

My other friend broke every mold in the book. She'd tie her long dreadlocks up in a knot on top of her head to slide under her motorcycle, fixing things most guys would be intimidated to even touch. She lived in tank tops, cut-off jean shorts, and flip-flops, and every guy on the block got shy and silly when Colby came around. She definitely wasn't manly, but she didn't try at all to be girly or beautiful. She just carried this peace about her—a confidence in who she was—that acted like a vortex to every guy who got too close. They were drawn to her but not threatened by her. They were intrigued by her mystery yet unafraid of her strength. Guys who had dated only models abandoned that physical standard to chase after shorter, edgy Colby because she humbly acted like a masterpiece that could be attained only by someone who recognized great art.

Our society teaches us that the more attractive you make yourself physically, the more people will be attracted to you. Unfortunately, this isn't the whole truth. It's only part of it. I know beautiful girls who are lonely because they're catty, tacky, and hard to be around, and I know very average-looking girls who are happily married, in relationships, and adored.

Romance might initially begin because of physical attraction, but love is sustained because of the heart.

For years I worked on my outer appearance because of this lie. I starved myself, checked mirror after mirror before leaving the house, and worked more on my reflection than on anything inside of me. The problem with this approach is that you don't end up living your life with a reflection. You spend your life with the person behind the exterior. You spend your moments with a personality beneath the skin. You live with the character inside the body. No matter how much Botox, liposuction, or plastic surgery you end up getting, at one point your body will eventually get old and wrinkly. Aging is inevitable. You can't spend every day in constant physical attraction, wanting to rip each other's clothes off. In fact, if you marry someone who is gorgeous but has no personality, believe me, it will last as long as the excitement of a passionate fling. It's not possible to spend the rest of your life having sex every minute of the day. You do extremely ordinary things: coexisting, grocery shopping, talking, bringing each other soup when you have the stomach flu, eating, sleeping, traveling, paying bills—going to the bathroom, for crying out loud.

The X-factor defies all physical attributes. It may be confidence, or it could be character. It might be inner peace or it might be humor. Whatever it is, it always trumps a perfectly immaculate appearance, especially if that immaculate appearance is the home of an ugly heart.

THE CHASE

I always dreamed of being chased by a guy, but I never thought it would happen. Any time a boy would show any interest, I would either come on too strong and scare him off, or beat him up verbally and then run for the hills. After I began choosing to intentionally see myself in a different light, guys were not only looking; they were coming around and wanting to stay.

This was new territory for me, but good territory. When my now Studhubs, Lucas, started chasing me, I wasn't sure if I wanted to be chased. I couldn't help but instantly drool over his perfect body, gorgeous face, and manly, rugged appearance. In fact, when we first started hanging out, girls would come up and slip him their phone numbers right in front of me. Talk about intimidating—and tacky.

Just a few months before I met him, any hot guy showing an interest in me not only would have swept me off my feet, but also would have been my dream come true. This newly worthy heart, however, was becoming more secure in what I deserved. I wanted to make sure there was more behind his deep blue eyes and long eyelashes that qualified him to be given the privilege of my fragile heart.

The first time he asked me out, I politely said no. This was definitely proof that something inside of me was changing. I'd only been asked out once in my entire life, so for me to say no was something I never thought possible. He was younger than I was, still figuring out what he wanted to do with his life, and I just wasn't sure we were headed in the same direction.

On top of that, I had this ridiculous list. My list consisted of things like, "has to be at least three years older than I am" and "needs to be at least six-four." As an extremely tall girl, I was determined not to be an Amazon woman (which I had been called before) or Keith and Nicole when I put on my high heels. The list was comprised of preferences, mostly from insecurities, but no list should ever be concrete parameters when looking for love. Love can surprise you in so many ways.

We had been hanging out a lot, and I was more than enjoying his company. But I didn't know if he was someone I was ready to commit to as more than a good friend, especially since he didn't perfectly match a few items on my beloved list.

My perspective, however, changed incredibly fast. One night while soaking in the bathtub, I made up an excuse to call my new friend with a very important question that, quite frankly, didn't need to be answered. When he picked up his phone and all I could hear were girls giggling in the background, I found my reaction strange. I was anything but happy. He asked if he could call me back later, obviously distracted by the party going on around him, and I sat there dumbfounded, rethinking my decision to say no to his romantic advances.

I sent a quick text, letting him know I might be reconsidering our constant hang-out arrangement. We seemed to be spending enormous amounts of time together each day, somehow always ending up at the same coffee shop— talking for hours at a time about everything under the sun.

My phone instantly rang.

"Christa," he said sternly, prefacing the weight of his

upcoming words. "I know you always have something to say, but I need you to be quiet for just a minute."

I sat in silence, nervously biting my lower lip, with no idea what was coming next.

"God doesn't show a man gold and give him silver. Well, I've found my gold, and it's you. I know you said you wouldn't go out with me, but I'm afraid I'm just not going to accept that. If you're not proud to walk into a room beside me because I'm younger than you, or because I'm not six-foot-four, then you don't know what kind of man I am. But I'd like to show you. I'm taking you out tomorrow night, so what time should I pick you up?"

The girl who always knew what to say was finally speechless. My heart was beating faster than it had ever beaten before. I felt a chill inside that was just as violent as the fear I'd always known but, in an eerie way, violently calm.

I knew at that very moment sitting in that bathtub, I had found the man worthy of holding my heart.

Just one short year and a whirlwind of a romance later, I was standing at the altar beside my best friend. He had chased me as a treasure, had fought for me as a protector, and had very quickly become the love of my heart. "Do you, Christa, take Lucas to be your lawfully wedded husband—to have and to hold from this day forward?"

I took a deep breath, attempted to calm my racing heartbeat, and with oceans of sincerity, spilled the two little words I had only dreamed of one day saying:

"I do."

The girl who had always found herself rejected, alone, and in the perpetual best-friend role was standing across from the man of her dreams, and not only was he in love; he was making a covenant in front of God, family, and friends, declaring his devotion for the rest of his life.

The dream was no longer just a dream. He was flesh and blood with tear-filled eyes in front of me.

He was finally here. I was head over heels. And it really was…perfect.

MOST PRECIOUS POSSESSION

We love the feelings of a youthful crush—that electricity pulsing through our bodies at the notion of a possible love interest. We love fairy-tale movie endings and the sleepless nights that occur in a budding romance. But after the lightning bolts and heart palpitations die down, there's always a dose of reality waiting at the door. Reality can sometimes be a harsh truth that dries up infatuation and causes lovesick emotions to vanish.

When you fall in love, you are entrusting someone to take care of your heart, and that person, in turn, is doing the same. If you choose to hand over the center of your being to someone you're extremely physically attracted to but who is known for bad character, the probability of that bad character seeping into your relationship is relatively high. If you decide to hand over your most precious treasure to someone who is known to be a player, but you just can't seem to keep away from those baby blues and sweet talk, your treasure might be one of many peas in that player's harem-like pod.

Our hearts are everything, my friends. Their condition determines every part of our existence—from friends and jobs to the effort and persistence we put into getting out of bed in the morning. Your heart shouldn't be given away to anyone who will take it—it shouldn't be thrown about and casually used and abused like a pair of old hand-me-downs. Your heart should be guarded and treasured as your most precious possession, a pearl of great price, a holy grail, an eighth wonder of the world.

Whoever you choose to give it to will hold and help

define a part of your destiny simply because you've given that person that power.

I'm definitely not suggesting that you lock up your heart in an iron vault and throw away the key because you're afraid it will get hurt. I am proposing, however, that you take a closer look at the weight and worth of your heart, since it is the most important part of your existence on this earth.

Looking back on my experiences as a kid, I'm actually grateful for some of the rejection I encountered in the early years. There's no telling what crazy things I would have done with all sorts of people who were unprepared and unqualified to protect me. I probably would have done just about anything with my body (and did to a certain extent) to feel loved and accepted in my soul, which is why I'm glad a lot of romantic doors in front of me remained barred shut. I now see parts of my rejection as a strange sort of protection.

Let me explain what I mean.

Sex and love are not the same thing. They are vastly different in their definitions, yet in our culture, the two seem to get thrown into the same pot and used interchangeably. If I could have, I'm positive I would have given away a whole lot of sex while looking for a whole lot of love in the early years—hoping to feel some sort of connection with anyone who would take me. But if I'd used sex like a worm on a hook to try and catch love, I would have consistently come up short. I've been the strong shoulder for many friends as they cried their eyes out in agony over giving themselves to people who disappeared after they got what they wanted in the bedroom.

Inside the parameters of love, sex is unsurpassable. It brings two people closer together than they ever could have imagined. But it doesn't create love. It enhances it.

There is such a thing as sex without love. It happens

every day all over the world, but for many reasons, this wasn't something that was ever of interest to me in my adult years. I didn't see the worth in getting physically naked with someone before I got emotionally and spiritually naked with that person. In fact, giving someone my body before I had time to figure out if he was worth getting involved with seemed unwise to one already so tattered. I found it hard to believe that my heart could stay unattached while doing something so unbelievably intimate, and I definitely couldn't see how confusing my emotions prematurely would help at all to decipher whether or not this person was someone I wanted to do life with.

This is not always the case, of course, but men tend to give love in hope of sex, and women tend to give sex in hope of love. Women want romance. We like to be swept off our feet. We like to squeal and cry at a good love story, letting our emotions take us on a ride.

But love isn't just a feeling. We reduce it to that one simple term so many times, finding that when feelings fade or wane for a time, it must be time to move on. Of course love involves feelings and emotions. That's the fun part, and a massive part of romance. But more than anything, true, lasting love is a choice. And sometimes the choice to love goes against every feeling inside of your gut.

When Studhubs and I get into a fight, no matter how big or small and no matter whose fault it is, we both have to make a conscious choice to put aside feelings of pride, and instead fight for peace and reconciliation. I'm a natural redhead with Irish blood that, in the beginning of our marriage, I used to justify my fiery temper. Stubbornness and pride made it very difficult for me to admit when I was wrong or say that I was sorry. But because love is slow to anger, I have to put aside my feelings of anger and choose love instead. Because love is patient and kind, I have to take a deep breath, refuse my need to always be right, and say I'm sorry when I'm wrong. Because love is not jealous or boastful and it does not demand its own way, I have to think of his needs over my own. Because love endures all things and is quick to ask for forgiveness, I have to learn to forgive when I've been hurt, and ask for forgiveness when I have wounded. Love and pride are sworn enemies, and they're impossible living under the same roof. True love absolutely never fails (1 Corinthians 13).

Yes, I'm certain that by that definition, love and sex are not the same thing.

Can you imagine if I tried to interchange "sex" with "love" in that context? Sex is slow to anger. Sex is patient and kind. Sex is not jealous or boastful—it does not demand its own way. Sex endures all things and is quick to ask for forgiveness. Sex keeps no record of wrong. Sex puts your needs before mine.

Doesn't really have the same pizzazz to it, does it? Most people think of sex as something they do with just their bodies. They view it as harmless and innocent—something you do when you want to feel good and have a good time. But the body isn't the only thing involved when two people are having sex. The heart is always affected in some way, even unconsciously, because the heart and soul are affected by every single thing that we do. Many people think the heart is something that can be turned on and off like a light switch—simply forgotten in this passionate act. Your heart can become numb over time, hardening with each meaningless giveaway, but I don't believe it can ever be turned off completely.

I wouldn't want it to.

You don't need to become a nun to protect and treasure your heart and soul. You don't need to lock on your iron chastity belt and throw away the key. You just need to be aware of the wealth that is inside of you, and to know that every time you choose to let your heart be captivated by the gaze of another, it's your job alone to make sure that person is someone worthy of holding your most precious possession. In order for you to flourish, the person you entrust your heart with has to be someone who wants to see it flourish as much as you do, and vice versa.

Take a deep, long look inside of yourself and see the worth, the gold, the potential, and the unique creativity that make up you.

And then feel empowered to be extremely picky in choosing the person you hand your gold over to.

WHOLENESS

I didn't go into my marriage entirely free from my eating disorder. I was eons away from rock bottom and was living in huge realms of freedom compared to my past, but there seemed to be a little demon on my shoulder that sometimes pricked me with his pitchfork, and I would run back to some of the same old addictive, destructive behaviors for a meal or two.

Remember how I mentioned at one point that I truly believed my husband would be so disappointed I had cellulite on my butt that he would divorce me? Well, my belief system when I entered my marriage might not have been as drastic as the dreadful "D" word, but I definitely believed he would be painfully disappointed and probably wouldn't tell me.

The first few months of our marriage were hilarious, in a dark-comedy kind of way. I felt more comfortable with the lights off and would always try to turn at a favorable angle or let him go through the door first if we happened to not have any clothes on. I'd jump if he came in while I was changing or throw the covers quickly over my exposed frame. But every single time he looked at me, he looked at me like he had won the lottery. He would bombard me with compliments, constantly telling me how beautiful I was, how blessed he was, and how I was the most gorgeous woman in the entire world. I knew he meant it. My husband doesn't always say much, so when he says something, there's a weightiness to his words.

He would always tell me, "Christa, I promise you. The second you stop obsessing and worrying about your weight and food, everything will align in order."

At first I didn't believe him. How could he know about these things? How in the world could not thinking about food help anything? Wouldn't I become a cow if I stopped worrying about food, eating anything and everything I wanted to eat? Fortunately for me, he never stopped pressing the issue, over and over, day in and day out. Eventually, and despite full assurance on my own part, my walls began to fall. The more he affirmed his unconditional love for me, and the less pressure there was on me to be a perfectly chiseled naked goddess, the more my body changed with little to no effort at all. I began eating things I never allowed myself to eat and actually enjoyed the food without guilt. I began skipping workouts to do things that I loved, instead of slaving away in devotion to this outward shell of a body that needed to be perfect but never was.

His constant IV drip of affection and adoration coursed through every part of me—plowing through my insecurity like a wrecking ball crashing into solid concrete, and because my head and heart were being released into freedom, my body was released into freedom.

As a result, I probably dropped twenty pounds with absolutely no effort—eating anything I wanted and just stopping when I was full. Because food had lost its bad factor, there was no longer any need to hide and binge. In fact, the first time Lucas caught me on a secret binge in front of the refrigerator, he picked up a bag of chips, put a smile on his face, and joined right in, saying, "Baby, there's no need to do this in secret anymore. There's nothing you can do that will make me love you any less than I do—so if you need to binge, let's binge together." Talk about taking the bullet out of the gun. And because everything was now permissible, I didn't have any reason to run to certain foods, since I could have them anyway. The more freedom I found with what I could eat, the more food had lost its binge appeal, and the more my weight evened out to what it naturally needed to be—just as God had intended.

Now, I know my husband is rare, which is why I hope he'll write a book for men someday on how to be a man and how to love your wife. I used to say, "I married the world's largest heart. He just happened to come in a hunky frame and looks like a Roman god." But, friends, you don't need to wait until you find a Studhubs, Superwife, Supergirlfriend, or Studboyfriend to start believing in yourself. In fact, if you get the wrong one, it could make things worse. You don't need to wait until you find your life partner to find yourself being loved into wholeness.

It can start right here. Right now. And it starts with loving yourself.

↓ YOUR TURN:
Loving Yourself

So we've talked about forgiving ourselves, letting ourselves off the hook, believing in ourselves, speaking words of truth and life about ourselves—everything we've heard but may not have done. We laugh at cheesy self-help books that tell us to love ourselves because it's hitting a subject extremely close to home, and it's way easier to respond with humor when we're uncomfortable with a concept we don't want to face. Believe me—I know.

This step is crucial to your house being healed and whole. You must love yourself to believe in who you are. You must love yourself to fully forgive yourself and see permanent change. You have to learn what it really means to look in the mirror and see a friend, not an enemy.

But first...

Once again, ask God to come in and fill up your leaky love bucket with His unconditional love.

Remember, you can give away only what you've first received. Whatever is primarily inside of your heart is what you're going to give, over and over again. Many of you can't love yourselves because you haven't allowed yourself to be loved.

Get quiet. Still your mind and silence those screaming thoughts of doubt and fear. Ask Unconditional Love to come in and hold you, embrace you, and heal you. Ask the perfect love of God to meet you where you are, with all your failures, mistakes, and shameful experiences. And now the most important part—you must receive it. Receive the gift of love and grace that none of us can ever earn, but that's always available. Let it wash over your wounds,

your abuse, your addictions, and your fears. Let it pour
into the dry cracks and bring life to old dry bones.

Bathe in it. Soak in it. Drink it in.

Stay here until you can physically feel it. I promise
you, it will come.

Now, out of the fullness of your love-saturated heart, write a love letter to yourself.

Include things that you admire or things that you're proud
of. Even if it's that you love yourself for not throwing in the
towel during this healing journey we've been on. That's a
start. Even if it's that you love yourself for not trying hard
enough when you hit rock bottom and attempted suicide.
You might love that you adore cats, or you might love how
you look in blue jeans. Find something, anything, and see
what comes out.

You might have to fake some things. I didn't necessarily fully believe that I was always worthy of love and gushing with admiration for myself while I was saying the words
into the rearview mirror that first day, but it got the ball
rolling. And I said them over and over until they stuck.

Go in front of the mirror with your list, look deep into your eyes, and tell yourself what you love about yourself.

You need to hear and see yourself saying these things. You
need to look in your eyes and hear with your ears what you
believe. Words create—especially your words. Don't worry
about feeling like an idiot—you'll be all alone. Just try it
and see what happens.

The results might surprise you.

The View

By Christa Black

Just unloaded the last box up two long flights of stairs
And I realized that everything I own is in this room
I don't know how I got here and I'm not sure where to start
If you asked me to retrace my steps, it would probably be too far
But I'm sitting on these wrinkled sheets and thinking to myself
I might be happy
And I just have to say

CHORUS:

The view looks fine from here
Everything seems nice this time of year
And even though the future is unclear
I might just stick around awhile

My landlord's name is Barbara and I sometimes call her Mom
Her Jersey accent reminds me just how far away from home I am
And I love the way the traffic keeps moving down below
Seems the people in this city always have someplace to go
And there are couples walking everywhere as I sit all alone
But I am happy
And I just have to say

CHORUS:

The view looks fine from here
Everything seems nice this time of year
And even though the future is unclear
I might just stick around awhile

BRIDGE:

'Cause the sun's about to rise
Oh, I've never seen it look so bright
I've waited all my life

Got a couple hundred dollars and an 8x16 room
Most people think I'm crazy—said I took off way too soon
But I can't describe this longing that's pulling me inside
Sometimes following your heart can be an interesting ride
But I'm looking over rooftops at the colors
And I know that I am happy

Chapter 9

The Destination

I peered out into the gray—jaw open, heart racing—fighting to keep my teeth from chattering loudly from the biting cold. I was right smack in front of a towering wall of blue glacier ice that made me feel more like a tiny ant in the middle of a cornfield than a girl accustomed to being the tallest. Complete strangers stood shoulder to shoulder on the bow of the ship with cameras poised and ready, every one of us feeling an instant kindred as we watched in silence, staring up into the glorious Alaskan expanse that swallowed up our boat in its beauty. The eleven-story cruise liner we boarded out of Seattle was anything but small, but even the largest of man-made creations would have paled in grandeur next to the magnificent terrain very few of us had ever seen before.

It felt as though we were trespassers on sacred waters—that any wrong move might be disrespectful and sacrilegious to the untouched frontier. I knew I was witnessing a sight so unbelievably majestic, I simply didn't know whether to laugh, cry, say a prayer, maybe clap and cheer, or just stop breathing altogether in reverence of the giant glacial force, strong enough to rearrange mountains.

We kept hearing what sounded like cracks of lightning in the distance, yet the clouds overhead seemed void of any thunderstorms. As each crash broke the silence, massive chunks of ancient ice broke loose, some as tall as skyscrapers, clapping loudly as they fell to freedom into the freezing ocean waters below.

Our cruise ship captain delicately navigated us safely through the foggy mountain bay. Whales jumped as if they knew we were watching, showing off their beautiful regality, seagulls swooped in to filch from unsuspecting guests holding on to unfinished food, and mountain streams trickled down to join their icy waters with the Pacific Ocean calm.

It was all just enough to make a girl lose her breath over and over again.

It felt so good to finally see the world with awe and wonder—and actually be grateful. It felt so powerful to explore the power of life around me. I was far from the girl who once felt that making it through the day was a feat more extraordinary than winning a gold medal in the Olympics. Survival had once been an art form that was a common necessity. It had been the only way to tackle the next breath or potentially just make it out of bed in the morning.

But I was far from surviving. I was living.

After years of black depression, the living hell of an eating disorder, and days drenched in hopelessness and insecurity, I stood as a woman with her head held high against the Alaskan winds, drinking in the breezes of freedom.

I squeezed Studhubs's hand as we looked out at the freezing waters of Glacier Bay. His presence beside me evoked affection and gratitude—knowing that he is a living, breathing, loving reminder of the woman I must have become to be chosen by such a man as he.

I'm far from the girl who once believed in her cage more than her freedom, who clung to rejection more than acceptance. I'm galaxies away from the magnetic pull of the endless buffet in the dining hall on the cruise ship. The addiction is miraculously forgotten for one who was once so violently addicted to food and other substances.

My heart has been seasoned and scarred in the perils of a bloody war for peace, but peace has most definitely been won, and each room inside got an extreme heart-edition makeover in the process.

When I look at my own reflection these days, I see so much more than another girl with another story. I see so much more than just a woman who survived the inevitable heart beatings of this life.

I see a survivor who has finally overcome.

And I see an overcomer who has learned what it truly means to be alive.

TRIALS

I'm not legally qualified with a diploma as a psychiatrist or a counselor to help others. I don't have my master's or PhD. I haven't read books on the brain or studied what scientists and doctors have researched. What qualifies me to help others is simply this: I know all about trial by fire. I've been through the wringer and come out on the other side.

You'd be crazy to sign up for the fire intentionally. No one likes obstacles, hardships, or mishaps—going bankrupt, getting a divorce, or losing someone dear. We might like what the fire produces in us after it's all over, but most people wouldn't volunteer for a flogging unless they had a few screws loose.

For most of my life, when I would get hit with a hard time, a tribulation, an addiction, or a heartbreak, I would do anything and everything to extract myself from the situation as quickly as possible. I'd run from the flames, call in the troops, search for the nearest exit sign, and find as many shortcuts as I could. The problem with this approach to the fire is this: You might not have learned everything you needed to learn in the midst of that trial, which means you will probably have to go through it again.

My friend Tyson is an incredible man. At the age of thirty, he's been married, cheated on, left, and then divorced. He has three beautiful kids, teaches at a school, is a pastor, brings students into his home to live with his family, and is more highly revered by those closest to him than anyone I've ever seen. I sat in his class one day as he talked about the knife-gashing agony that divorce brings to the heart. His wife had left him for another man with little or no explanation, got pregnant, and had another baby, and his once happy home shattered into shards of broken glass around him.

You would think that he would have all sorts of amazing tips about how to overcome heartache faster, or ten steps to healing that will get you back on your feet in a jiffy. And while he has written a book on the power of forgiveness and healing after a deep betrayal, his wise words to us that day in class were far beyond his years.

He told us to embrace the suffering.

Now, at first, I flinched, as did most of the class. Embrace suffering? What kind of a masochistic teaching was this, anyway? What kind of person wants to throw their arms around misery and give it a hug? But the more he talked, the more truth I heard, and the more he didn't sound so crazy after all.

I wonder sometimes how much further along I would have been if I had learned this concept sooner. What if during every hard season I had stopped to ask myself the question, "Okay, what do I need to learn from this so I never have to go through it again?" instead of, "How the heck can I avoid this bullet and get the heck out of Dodge?"

I've been in lots of relationships, business deals, family feuds, friend betrayals, church backstabbings, and countless situations that brought more agony than a dump truck full of cow manure being poured out on my head. I'm sad to say that in most of these circumstances, I simply ran for my life. I'd leave beaten and torn, tattered and wounded—crawling through the mud for the nearest safe place. It wasn't really until last year that I started sitting down in the midst of a war and learning how to rest. I started looking at agony, fear, pain, and misery and saying, "All right, buddy—you're here, and I'm not running. What character can I take away from this pain? What strength can I glean from remaining still in the middle of a storm? What power can I obtain by learning how to stand in the heat of battle?"

The moment I started practicing this principle, the trials didn't seem so big anymore. They weren't pleasant by any means, but I loved who I became in the midst of them, and I loved that I could always find something to be joyful about—even in the worst situation.

I used to wish for a magic pill to end the suffering of my eating disorder. Our country is one of the most medicated countries in the world, popping all sorts of pills that offer instant gratification for symptoms and not problems. I am not against the extraordinary advances in medication; in fact, I think it's phenomenal how medicine has helped millions cope and find healing. I don't, however, believe that medication for emotional issues should be seen as the cure—especially in terms of depression. Medication can be a vital helper that gets you stable enough to then find healing, but it should never be seen as a permanent solution to a deeper problem.

I always hoped that one of my fervent prayers would result in a bolt of lightning able to zap me into wholeness. I begged for it, cried out for it, even screamed at God to come down in a chariot of fire and rescue me from this horrific pit. And in His wisdom, He did help deliver me and illuminate truth in such a way that I actually got to be a part of the process. He took my hand and walked with me out of the fire—three steps forward, two steps back. Three steps forward, two steps back.

I learned His kindness and mercy, His gentleness and faithfulness, and His power and strength in the process of extreme pain.

Oh, I totally believe He could have kissed my boo-boo and made it all better instantly, but instead, He led me gently into the past, into the dark places of wounding, and began to heal the trauma—one terrible memory at a time. I got to be a part of the healing and I changed along the journey.

When you experience trauma, a part of you stays right there, stunned by the experience, unable to grow and mature. I had fragments of my soul that were still stuck as that little six-year-old crying on the playground or the teenager consumed by rejection at the dance or the child who had been touched in a sexual way. A part of your soul literally stops growing in certain areas where trauma has occurred. Until you go back to the suffering and embrace the pain and ask for healing, you might stay that little six-year-old in certain areas.

But I don't want my soul to be fragmented from the past. I want to be healed and whole in every area of my life. I'm truly becoming that woman every day.

And you can become healed and whole too.

THE JOURNEY

My Studhubs and I recently drove up through the winding Northern California Cascade Mountains to the beautiful green of Oregon for a Fourth of July weekend celebration with friends. Paul Young and his family are probably most well-known for his number one *New York Times* best seller *The Shack*, but in our lives, they're definitely best known for their love, support, and amazing friendship.

I feel like I should probably keep a pen and paper

hidden under the table when I'm with him, so I can scrib-ble notes as he casually blurts out nuggets of gold while thumbing through a mental Rolodex filled with all sorts of random treasures. The wisdom that pours from his mouth is astounding and always challenging.

I sat in Paul's beautiful office, which is filled with all sorts of books that are rich in all sorts of knowledge, with walls covered by original art painted by those whose lives were changed by his story, and with little wooden shack replicas adorning desks and hanging off bookshelves. He played me a few songs from his favorite CD, and we sat and chatted for a bit—a luxury many would pay money for. Certain passing sentences flew out so fast and hit me so hard, I almost wanted to ask him to give me a minute while the weight of his words sank deeply into my soul.

"The journey is the destination, Christa," he said softly. "The process you're in is the goal. Success is never defined by the outcome, but by the process."

The weight of his words hit me like a jar of honey, slowly and warmly pouring sticky-sweet over my heart and soul.

Most of my life had been lived for a future day. I dreamed, planned, and wrote out goals. I looked forward to greater conquests and was always anticipating what was just around the bend. Those are all good things, of course, but not when you're missing today in expectation of tomorrow.

I know a guy who won a Super Bowl ring. He said that after the game was over, after the bottles of champagne had been uncorked and the cheers had silenced in the stadium, he stumbled upon a very strange emotion. What should have been the crowning moment of his life, reach-ing the pinnacle of any football player's career, lasted only a brief moment. He headed home after the game, took a shower, and got into bed, and an unexpected sadness came over him. He had reached the absolute top of the mountain he had fought his entire life to climb and conquer, and the top was fantastic for a minute, but once he reached the peak, there were no more mountains up ahead to climb. There wasn't more territory to conquer in his field. He had reached the moment he had always dreamed would fulfill him for the rest of his life, but instead, once the moment was gone, he felt vastly empty.

During my eating disorder years, I would stand high on my tiptoes, straining to see the light of freedom. When I was single, I believed if I could just fall in love and get married, all of my heart problems would instantly be solved. When I did fall in love and get married, I became restless in the little apartment we had once been so content with and thought, "If only we can get the place we want, then we'll really have made it." When we got the loft that we loved, it was too small. When my first album came out, I believed that if a label, manager, or booking agency would just pick up the album, or if I could just land my big break somehow, then I'd find perfect peace. While I was touring with other artists in a supporting role for years, I simply thought, "If I can just get that microphone in my own hands, my universe will finally be in order."

How many precious moments of my journey have I missed while out in search of a future destination?

Every mountaintop I conquer always reveals another mountain waiting to be climbed and taken. There will always be another goal to obtain, another view to behold, and something bigger and better up ahead that can keep a rumbling of discontent deep in my gut. If I do reach my highest goal and believe that moment will bring me peace for the rest of my life, I'll be painfully disappointed, just like my Super Bowl ring–wearing friend.

Here's what I've learned that brings me incredible peace: I can rest right where I am today in the journey, knowing that if this is where I am, it's exactly where I need to be. I can have hope for tomorrow, but not at the expense of missing the now moments that I can never get back. I drink deeply of the cup of contentment today, no matter how bad my circumstances are, as I wait for the future sun.

And I've committed to stop searching for the gold of another day, and start holding on to the treasure that's already within my hands.

TREASURE HUNTERS

I'm learning to be a treasure hunter, but not in the ways I formerly would have imagined. Instead of always search-ing for the golden egg up ahead, the next high, the greater mountaintop, or the secret formula to happiness and eter-nal bliss, I'm learning to find priceless treasures in the life that I hold in my hands at this very moment.

I'm finding such joy in the simple things these days—gratitude for my loving family, which has always supported me in my ludicrous ventures; sinking into my nightly hot bath, letting the day soak away; searching for the world's perfect cup of coffee; and watching Studhubs cooking for me in the kitchen.

I looked down at my beautiful violin today, the same one that has been with me for more than twenty-two years, admiring the intricate details the German violin maker took such care and attention to create while making this instrument that has traveled with me all over the world. How many times have I taken for granted the wood, bow, and strings that have been such a blessing to so many—how my great-grandmother Amy left an inheritance to my grandfather, then passed it down to my mother, who decided to invest that money in a beautiful violin for her only daughter. That inheritance has changed my life and blessed millions of strangers in the process.

There are more moments just waiting to be claimed treasures than there are grains of sand. We miss them every day, sometimes hundreds and thousands of times. The familiar should never become too familiar. A quick acknowledgment of a treasure is just as powerful as a detailed log or a promise to remember. In fact, it would be impossible to remember them all. But every acknowledgment of a treasured moment goes with you, growing like a snowball rolling down a hill. The power and force become impossible to ignore as you carry the gold of these moments and add them to the wealth of your life.

Gratitude brings freedom. When freedom becomes reality, we are able to fully live. Living free from worry, anxiety, depression, fear, and addiction is living with the riches that very few ever fully attain.

My life is extremely wealthy. I have room after room in my heart filled with costly jewels that have absolutely nothing to do with money or possessions. I'm thankful in the harvest, and I'm thankful in the drought, and there is treasure in both extremes. You just have to know how to look for it. In fact, most of my invaluable wealth was accumulated in the lean seasons, obtained only when I was thrown into the fire.

When silver is refined by heat and flame, the impurities inside the metal rise to the surface. The silversmith takes great care in scraping the unwanted substance out of the shimmering mass, making sure the substance is purified. As we find ourselves in the fire, the ugly, the impatient, the prideful, the shameful, and the cruel rise to the surface, but this isn't necessarily a bad thing. The more impurities are extracted from the silver—surrendered to God, allowing Him to purify us through His love—the more precious the metal becomes.

I long to be the proud owner of a costly, fulfilled,

wealthy treasure of a life. I want the junk out of my heart. I want to be purified. I long to see others discover the worth inside of themselves and in the hearts that beat within their chests—no matter what life-beatings have come and gone.

There's always more healing. There's always more hope.

And there's always more treasure to be found in every moment of this precious life that we hold—just waiting to be discovered and claimed.

▼ YOUR TURN:
Destination/Process

We all go through tough seasons. They're impossible to avoid in this bumper-car life. Is there a situation that you've been running from or trying to get out of that you might need to stop and face? You might have trouble with authority, causing you to keep losing your job. You might be in a pattern of being dumped or cheated on. You could consistently find yourself broke or in trouble with money. You might be walking through a sickness or dealing with the death of a loved one. Getting another job won't fix your problem, nor will finding another boyfriend, and neither will a winning lottery ticket. Worrying about your illness won't heal you, and staying angry won't bring your loved one back. Your problems don't just go away, especially if you see a pattern forming.

Is there a trial that you need to turn around and face head-on?

Turn around and face the problem you're in. Stop running from it, and look it in the eyes. What do you need to learn from this trial that you can't learn anywhere else? Is this trial chasing you because you're running? Does your lying keep getting you into trouble? Does your gossip keep attracting drama? Is your bank account always empty? Are you at rock bottom? Turn around and confront the hard time, and find out why it's allowed to be there. If it's your fault, face the reality of what's inside of you that might need to change. If it's not your fault, don't run from the fire. Glean everything you can from the situation to make you a better person within the flames. The fire might not immediately change, but you will change inside the fire.

Are you in search of a destination at the expense of the journey?

When we're in high school, we can't wait until we get to college, and when we're in college, we can't wait to get out and get our first job. When we get our first job, we can't wait until we get married, and when we get married, we can't wait until we have children. Once we have children, we can't wait until we get the bigger house, and once we get the bigger house, we can't wait to get the vacation house. Once we get the vacation house, we can't wait to retire.

There will always be a bigger and better destination up ahead. Always.

Have you stopped enjoying the journey? Have you forgotten what today holds in expectation of the next best thing?

I find over and over in my own life that I become the person I need to be in the season I'm going through. If I had been handed my own platform, my own microphone, and my own show three years ago, it would have absolutely destroyed me. Why? Because I wasn't the person I needed to be—yet.

For ten years I toured with an incredible man and artist named Michael W. Smith. He was far more than a boss—I lived with his family for years, his children have become as close as siblings to me, and I would do just about anything for them. I was so ready to get my own microphone and have my own platform that I quit his band four times to try to go make my own way. Every time I'd jump out of the boat, he'd let me go (being the gracious, wise, loving man that he is), always believing in me as I paddled away. But every single time, without fail, I'd eventually come back. Why?

I wasn't ready yet.

My character wasn't ready. My heart wasn't healed. If I had obtained my own microphone and my own stage, I would have stood up with absolutely nothing relevant to say. I would have pointed people to myself and hoped for fame, but I wouldn't have done anything truly significant. I would have sung another pretty song and played another nice tune, but in my opinion, the world doesn't need another good song. The world needs people who know who they are, standing in their true identity, releasing something unique into people's lives. I refuse to just sing another meaningless song, I want to sing something life-changing to the world, but I couldn't sing that song until I had lived that song.

How many people get to the destination prematurely and aren't who they need to be in order to stay there?

Our lives are such journeys. If we ever really arrived, we might actually be at the end. Instead of seeing certain moments as throwaway days to get me to my next destination, I'm beginning to look at every day as the destination, no matter what situation I might find myself in.

The journey is the destination, my friends. Embrace it, face it—squeeze every last drop of wisdom, experience, and knowledge out of every situation you face. I'm learning to embrace the process, hard or easy, fun or miserable. I've been in some heartbreaking situations, and I don't run from them anymore. I beat their punches by swinging back, by fighting to stand, by contending to keep my heart soft and at peace in the midst of adversity, and by taking every single treasure I can from the journey. I sigh deeply with gratitude in the good times, and sigh deeply in gratitude that I will overcome the bad.

My heart goal is to become the best I can become. I'm training my eyes to see the wealth in everything I face, large or small, fantastic or devastating. We're all on such a fast ride, and we get only one ticket. I'm determined to finish well, to stand up again after a fall, to cry my eyes out when my heart breaks, to taste the newness of experiences, and to savor the familiar in deep gratitude and contentment. I've committed to live louder, to love deeper, and to jump off more cliffs, regardless of whether I know if there's a river down below to catch my fall.

Life. What a delicious gift, if we allow ourselves to truly taste its flavors.

Epilogue

Insight into Nutrition

My dear friend Dr. Simone Laubscher is a renowned doctor who lives in London. I met her for the first time at the recommendation of a friend who said she had met with someone who was helping to treat eating disorders and cancer through diet and nutrition, which, of course, immediately piqued my interest. I walked into my first appointment to find a gorgeous young blonde with a zeal for life and a laugh to match, making me double-check the name on the door to see if I'd accidently picked the wrong room. Shouldn't big, important doctors be old men with long faces in boring white coats?

Simone has proved to be anything but boring in my life.

I called her up to ask for her expertise on the matter of nutrition as it pertains to eating disorders, and while managing her full-time clinic in London, opening two new clinics in Cairo and Barbados this year, creating and manufacturing a line of unbelievably delicious gluten-free products, and being an amazing wife and mother of two babies with another on the way, she still found time to give me some info, and here's what I got.

Most binge eaters don't understand that carbohydrates and starches (such as cakes, cookies, and breads) begin digesting in the mouth with an enzyme called salivary amylase. Before the food even hits the stomach, it's already being digested—going straight into the bloodstream. With carbohydrates being the go-to binge choice, their extremely high glycemic index makes a person's blood sugar surge initially, only to plummet after about thirty minutes, leaving the person feeling completely exhausted. I knew this pattern well—bingeing heavily on carbs only to crash very shortly thereafter, both physically and emotionally.

The hellish cycle of bulimia and overeating is one that never ends. The binger is always chasing and longing for another rush after each binge, and sometimes purge. When the food intake is too much to handle, it must be thrown up. Then the binger crashes with his or her blood sugar. But after the rush from the binge leaves and the body hasn't received the nutrients it needs to function, another rush is needed. The cycle continues, round and round, over and over again. You swear this binge and purge will be your last time, but physically and chemically, you're making it almost impossible to win the battle.

Vitamin and mineral levels become depleted in the body as a result of the poor food choices and the fact that you're throwing up most of your food. Because the body isn't receiving the nutrients it needs to function properly, cravings increase. This, compounded with low blood-sugar levels, leaves a person fighting uncontrollable cravings.

"You see, your body doesn't know that there's a twenty-four/seven supermarket down the road, so it's going to go into survival mode when it doesn't get the food it needs," says Laubscher. "Once that happens, you're going to have one heck of a fight on your hands."

Our bodies are extremely smart and geared toward survival—even if our choices are not. Eating disorders, however, go against that survival instinct. They are, instead, a slow form of suicide. When our bodies aren't getting the nutrients and fuel they need to survive, they will scream the message through cravings, crashing blood sugar, headaches, emotional overloads, fatigue, and exhaustion. You basically feel insane and unstable—all the time.

Most bulimics don't choose proteins as their first choice in a binge. If it was between a packet of turkey and a packet of Twinkies, you better believe I went for the Twinkies. Bulimics usually go for the carbs: the box of cookies, the dozen donuts, the bag of chips, the pan of brownies, anything in the vending machine. Because proteins aren't usually ingested in a binge, there isn't any communication between the stomach and the brain. The body needs carbs and proteins for the brain to register that the stomach is full and it's time to stop eating. When the body is overloaded with only carbs, then purged, the blood sugar rises with the binge, then crashes violently, telling the brain that the body is even hungrier than it was before the binge began. The appetite then goes crazy, and believe me—you feel crazy right along with it.

Proteins and good fats are also released into your bloodstream more slowly than carbs. When food is eaten slowly, the brain gets the message loud and clear that the body is full, and you end up putting the fork down, feeling satisfied.

"This is actually key for someone to physically win over bulimia," says Laubscher. "If you switch to protein at each meal (such as eggs, fish, chicken, seeds, nuts, pulses/beans, and so on), choose a good fat (such as olive oil, olives, avocado, or low-fat cheese), and chew each mouthful approximately twenty times, your tummy and brain will start to get the right messages. You will be able to make good choices, and then lose the desire to binge."

On top of everything else, restricting, bingeing, and purging can slow down and ruin the body's metabolism. Your metabolism involves a complex network of hormones and enzymes that not only converts food into fuel, but also affects how efficiently you burn that fuel. Your metabolism is also influenced by your age, sex, heredity, and proportion of lean body mass. So more muscle means higher metabolism.

Think of your metabolism like a fire.

When you skip meals and stop putting fuel onto the fire, the flame gets low and reduces your body's ability to burn what needs to be burned. When I thought I was being good by skipping breakfast (because I had binged the day before and was trying to "fix" my mistake), my body would go into starvation mode and my metabolism would go down. With my metabolism then lower, my body would store my lunchtime meal as fats and not burn the calories as fuel. I had taught my body and my metabolism that food was inconsistent, so when it would get food, it would store it on my thighs, butt, and tummy because it didn't know when the next meal was going to come. I had trained it to be that way.

Now let's talk about what all this up-and-down roller-coaster riding does to your brain. As the blood sugar rises and falls with your food intake, your neurotransmitter serotonin gets severely depleted. This isn't really something you want lacking in your body.

"Serotonin is often called our 'happy molecule' and is responsible for making us feel happy and full of joy," says Dr. Laubscher. "When your 'happy molecule' becomes lacking, you obviously become more prone to depression, low self-esteem, self-loathing, which are all classic emotions that come with bulimia and anorexia."

At the height of my eating disorder, I never made the connection between my depression and the chemical and nutritional makeup of my body. I never bridged the two concepts together or concluded that one might be helping fuel the other—but they were completely, absolutely, positively tied together. That is why Dr. Laubscher sees patients every day who are now able to tackle the emotions of their eating disorder as she helps them regulate their food intake and blood-sugar imbalance. Once she's devised a program based on her ten-point biomarker system, used to crack each patient's metabolic code, finding stabilization through the nutrients the body needs, it's much easier for the person to tackle the emotional roots behind the addiction because the physical body is no longer screaming for the food that it needs. She successfully treats patients all over the world through in-person appointments, on Skype (don't we all love technology?), or over the phone, and has also written books and teaching CDs entitled *Free to Live from Depression, Free to Live at the Size You Want,* and *Free to Live from Cancer* (www.rejuv .co.uk).

Dr. Laubscher has helped me in so many ways to finally find freedom from the cycle of bulimia, anorexia, and overeating, and if you just happen to be in London, I highly suggest popping in for a visit (or a hug). If not, email her clinic for a Skype consultation or find a nutritionist or therapist in your area.

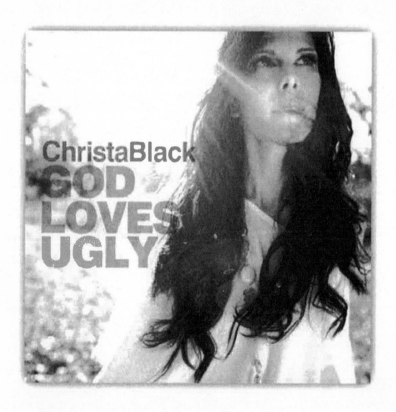